OUR BEST TOMORROW

Students Teaching Capitalism to America

Lauren Hudson
& Robert D. Hudson

Our Best Tomorrow
Students Teaching Capitalism to America

by Lauren Hudson & Robert D. Hudson

Illustrations by Robert Daniel Hudson

copyright ©2014 Lauren Hudson & Robert D. Hudson

To order additional copies of this book or for book publishing information, or to contact the author:

Headline Books, Inc.
P.O. Box 52
Terra Alta, WV 26764
www.headlinebooks.com

Tel: 800-570-5951
Email: mybook@headlinebooks.com

Cover design by Kevin T. Kelly, www.kevinkelly.com
Photography by J.H. Bolden

ISBN: 978-0-938467-92-2

Library of Congress Control Number: 2013952792

PRINTED IN THE UNITED STATES OF AMERICA

Patsy Hudson—
mother and grandmother—
an unsung hero

Table of Contents

PART 4 – IT'S TIME TO LEAD!

PART 5 – GET YOUR GAME ON!

Foreword

We present the second book in our series addressing capitalism and American exceptionalism. My daughter Lauren, age 13, wrote most of the business fable portions of this book. We hope it's a simple read which covers the basics of capitalism, albeit in a rather unconventional way, by blending business fables with direct teaching of business concepts.

I wrote the first book, *A Better Tomorrow: Fighting for Capitalism and Jobs in the Heartland*, from the perspective of a business advocate. As an attorney, I make a living trying to use words, facts, logic and, at times, emotion, to persuade. With a student book, the rhetoric had to be toned down, which is probably a good thing.

In *Our Best Tomorrow* we hope to connect with students through something other than dry accounts of capitalism. Capitalism only seems dry if you write or talk about it that way. It's actually about our hopes, dreams, successes, and failures. It's the America I grew up in as a Baby Boomer.

We studiously avoided political parties and labels in this book. Parties adjust and change over time. Both parties have gotten it right and wrong. If students understand principles and simple truths, they'll make the right choices.

Why the fascination with capitalism? This imperfect system brought America the highest standard of living in history. Patriotic Americans would naturally strive to understand the basics of capitalism, wouldn't they? Instead, capitalism has become one of America's most misunderstood concepts.

You may remember the December 2011 Pew Foundation study found that nearly 50 percent of Americans ages 18 to 29 view socialism positively and capitalism negatively. The need for further instruction on capitalism has become clear. A legitimate economic system will maximize *opportunities* for success, as a means of minimizing poverty and chronic failure. Over the long haul, despite setbacks, capitalism has been successful.

Capitalism consists of millions of ongoing "experiments" in business and life. Some of these experiments fail miserably. Others yield things like laptop computers, smart phones, and inventions which provide real jobs and change lives. It's the spirit upon which we built America. Government control, on the other hand, reduces the number of "experiments," which eventually curbs progress.

Those who favor centralized government control focus on the inherently pessimistic task of planning for failure. As we now know, by stifling innovation, centralized government control leads to failure *en masse.* Choosing centralized government involves surrendering our lives to a flawed concept – one where hope and work ethic gradually fade as time passes. The reason this happens is very simple. Centralized government control diminishes two primary motivators in life – both the stick (failure) and the carrot (success).

With the stick, think of capitalism and free markets as the nudge we need to overcome obstacles in our professional lives and, at times, in our personal lives. We prosperous Americans, like all relatively affluent societies before us, have a propensity to drift. With capitalism nudging us, we can overcome obstacles in our professional lives. We can become stronger and better equipped to cope with challenges in our personal lives.

With the carrot, you might say that capitalism is tailor-made for the energy or youth, with our whole lives ahead of us. In our youth, we have keener abilities to dream of success. Teaching capitalism better will help our youth lay the groundwork for success in their lives. With freedom, optimism can become a self-fulfilling prophecy. Our nation's best tomorrow will come when future generations choose to embrace this optimistic life path.

Capitalism's basic principles can be quickly taught to bright middle school students, high school students, and adults. God has blessed our family with two children who perform at high academic levels. They attend excellent public schools in Northern Kentucky, one of the most pro-business regions in the country. Unfortunately, not all our schools focus extensively on job creation, capitalism, and businesses.

It's one thing to have a sense that things aren't right. It's another thing to write a book about it. An event on Election Day 2012 convinced me to start working on this book. I visited a crowded local pizza restaurant for lunch. Government insurance mandates would soon lead many restaurants to reduce the hours of their workers below thirty a week. The 2012 election carried high stakes for restaurant workers and their management.

A nice customer asked the pizza restaurant's 20-something manager if he had voted. The manager glibly volunteered that he had no idea how he would vote. He added the politically correct comment that he had an open mind. In short, with a few hours left to vote, he had no clue. If we asked him how to make pizzas, he wouldn't equivocate or change his mind with each pizza he baked. If he did, we'd re-think his intelligence and value as a manager.

The kind customer said to the twenty-something pizza manager what everybody says. She responded that everybody should vote and that he really must do so because it's his duty. Her advice made me a bit uncomfortable. With this level of inattention, he would probably vote for the "coolest" candidate. For some reason, today's youth don't consider pro-business candidates to be cool. Sometimes even managers don't understand capitalism.

Reality set in. The uninformed will continue to vote and kind people will keep encouraging them to do so. Meanwhile, if we don't understand capitalism we have zero ability to connect higher taxes, increased regulation, and massive government debt with lost opportunities. At times our youth just know things aren't perfect and, I suspect, many of them are dreamers who vote for government to fix more things. This sounds simple and good, but it's not.

Blaming our youth won't help. They attended school for thousands of hours and we didn't teach all of our youth about this basic area of life. Additional instruction on capitalism and private sector job creation is our best hope. We want this book to serve as another tool in the tool box for teachers and parents.

If we can deliver education on capitalism like never before, we might see an amazing, somewhat ironic, turnaround. Think about it. What if our newly educated youth kick it into high gear and show a generation or two of adults the way?

Robert D. Hudson
September 30, 2013

Part One
We Begin As Students

1

Let's Get It Started

This book explains how capitalism creates wonderful opportunities which help make our country great. Lauren Hudson, a bright student, wrote most of the book's stories. Her father, Rob Hudson, a business leader, wrote most of the points on capitalism. You will read the ideas of a student and the thoughts of an older leader.

Why read this book? Because understanding capitalism can change your life. You will better understand businesses and most business people. You will know more about the world around you, seeing it differently. Some parts of capitalism may sound boring, but as you read the book's stories, we hope you will agree that capitalism is anything but boring.

Let's get it started with the basic idea. Capitalism is when a person strives to own all or part of business. It's also called free enterprise. Some people own their own businesses. Most adults in America at least own "shares" of business stock through their retirement funds. Each share is a small portion of a business. People from all walks of life own stocks – teachers, plumbers, janitors, and business executives. Some people are "capitalists" and they don't even know it!

Why is learning about this important? It's far bigger than the shares of stock we may own. Our jobs come from capitalism.

Most families have at least one family member who works about eight hours a day or more in a job. She may spend half her waking hours getting ready for work, going to work, working, and going home from work.

Isn't it important to understand what you may spend half your time doing and how it fits into our country? We will want to do everything we can to make the best of our "work" hours. We will want to earn more money and have more opportunities to help our family. Healthy capitalism can make this happen.

As you'll learn in this book, in the end, most of the "things" we have in life come from capitalism. Our money comes from capitalism. Money can't buy happiness, but not having any can tend to make life a much bigger struggle. If we don't understand capitalism, we will be confused, or worse, we can get left behind with that part of our lives.

This book explains why capitalism is not just about the "things" we buy – it can be a big part of our happiness. Many students and adults don't understand capitalism in this way, which is unfortunate because capitalism is very, very simple.

After reading this simple book, you will know more about capitalism than most people in our entire country. As you'll see from the experiences of our heroes Adelaide, Jake and Isabella, in the stories below, capitalism is about our everyday lives, with ordinary people doing extraordinary things.

We hope that everyone who reads this book will find other students and adults in their lives and maybe even teach them a thing or two about capitalism. If you do, who knows, you just might help them and help our country to have its best tomorrow. Please join us!

They Said It Long Ago...

Capitalism Works - "Doing well is the result of doing good. That's what capitalism is all about."
—American Author Ralph Waldo Emerson

Capitalism Leads The Way - Some see capitalism as a target to be shot and killed, others see it as somebody else's cow to be milked, but it's really "a sturdy horse pulling our wagon."
—British Prime Minister Winston Churchill
(paraphrased)

Capitalism Is Successful - "Only when the human spirit is allowed to invent and create, only when individuals are given a personal stake in ...benefiting from their success — only then can societies remain economically alive, dynamic, progressive, and free!"
—President Ronald Reagan

2

Adelaide Departs For A Land of Opportunity

Bon'jour fellow Americans! My name is Adelaide. It's nice to see that you have made it to the New York location of my world-wide clothing store, Summer in Paris. Not only does my store sell trendy American clothes – we sell accessories straight from my hometown of Paris!

Summer in Paris has at least one location in nearly every state in the US and in several other countries. Making my business so successful worldwide has been hard work. But let me tell you something – I've had more fun, traveled more places, and met more great people than I could ever have imagined. My life has been an adventure, but it wasn't always like that.

I will start by telling you a little about my childhood. I was born in a small apartment on the edge of Paris, France. Our life in France was difficult. My father worked in construction and there wasn't much work. He didn't go to college and came from a poor family.

My baby sister, Celeste, came into the world 5 years after I was born and things became a bit complicated. You see, my sister was a very ill child. She was born with an irregular heart and my parents believed that she wouldn't make it past the first year of her life. Dad wasn't working all the time. When he did work, lots of our money went to help Celeste. She wasn't getting much better.

One day, when I was about 9, my mother and father came home with my baby sister in my mother's arms. "Pack your bags, we're leaving!" my father ordered me. Tears threatened to spill over his eyes and onto his cheeks, but he held them back. At the time, I really didn't understand what was going on or why we were leaving, but without hesitation, I rushed to my room and threw all my belongings in my suitcase. I could hear my mother and father whispering in the room next to mine.

"Are you sure there is a place in America where there are jobs and where we can get her better help? We are leaving our home!" I could hear the agony in my mother's cracking voice and I recall becoming confused. Where is America? Could they really cure Celeste? Would we be able to get there in time? What if she doesn't make it?

I took one last look at our small apartment which was my home. I sat down one last time on the fluffy bedspread and sighed. I picked up my teddy bear that I slept with every night and held him in my arms, holding him tight.

"Sweetie, we have to leave. Now! We're going to make a better life for this family!" My mother sounded excited, but mostly she sounded desperate. I did not argue, how could I? I rose slowly, grabbed my suitcase, and turned to take one last look. I tried to capture the scene in my head. I wanted to remember it forever. I felt my mother tap me on the shoulder, as I turned to follow her out the front door.

I took a deep breath and stepped out the door, knowing that I would not be coming back for a long, long time. I left the only home I ever knew. It would be quite awhile before I really understood why they called America "the land of opportunity."

3

You Won't Keep Isabella Down!

"No! I told you that the red glass needs to be mixed with the blue glass, not the green one!"

Oh, hello, I didn't realize that you were coming so early! I'm Isabella. I'm sorry that it is so messy around here. Oh, watch that glass right there! One of my workers dropped a beautiful plate and it shattered everywhere. I hope you will enjoy your tour of the newest manufacturing facility of Glamorous Glass. As you probably noticed, I manufacture many different glass items, such as plates, cups, bowls, windows, tables, and even some jewelry.

People all over the United States and other countries buy my products and I could not be more proud of our business. We provide good jobs for lots of families. Growing up, my family wasn't the most successful family, so I have always wanted a better life for everybody's children. You see, I was happy and life seemed perfect until I got the news that changed my life forever.

I heard a knock on the front door to my house and I ran to grab it. I flung the door open only to see a man in a police uniform holding a white envelope in his hands. His face was sullen and quiet. "Bella, who's at the door?" My mom called from upstairs. When I didn't answer her, she came down to see what was wrong. She managed to stifle a gasp when she saw the strange man standing in our doorway.

"Hello, are you, Mrs. Waters?" the man asked in a deep, husky voice.

"Yes," she whispered. The man held out the letter to her and fear filled her deep green eyes. She took it with a shaking hand and opened it. The man turned and walked away and I shut the door behind him.

"What does it say, Mommy?" I asked her, curious. Tears began to stream down her cheeks and she looked up at me.

"He's gone. Daddy's gone…. And he's not coming back, baby," she whispered, drawing me in her arms. At first, I didn't understand what she meant, but then a light bulb clicked.

"Did Daddy go to heaven?" I asked her, afraid of the answer.

"Yes, baby. Yes he did." She struggled with the words, practically choking them out. As I realized that he was dead, I too began to cry. We sat there, in each other's arms for awhile before the tears stopped flowing. But I knew that even though the tears had stopped for now, my mother was not okay, and neither was I.

It felt like we lost everything that day. Our small family of three had dwindled to just two. She lost her husband, her love, the person she could tell anything to and trust with her life. I lost a father, a caregiver, somebody who always told me to be strong and helped me back up when I fell.

I couldn't imagine at the time just how much this loss would affect us. My mom went into a deep depression about a week after his death. She stopped working, stopped cleaning, stopped cooking, and stopped caring for me at all. Over time, money became scarce and I didn't know what would happen to me or my mother. We no longer had the money to buy new clothes or new shoes.

I walked to school every day, but even school wasn't an escape from horrible memories and tears. I was teased. I was ridiculed. I was picked on all because of the way I looked and the way I dressed. Sure, I wasn't like the other kids and I was different in some ways, but that gives them no right to pick on me!

By the time I reached third grade, I had learned to tune it out. I didn't care what they thought. You see, I knew that one day I would be on top! I would work harder. I would be smarter. I would make a way in this world. Sure, there were days when I thought my best tomorrow would never come. But you see, I decided on my own - nothing would keep me down!

4

Talent, Passion and Freedom Make Jake A Winner!

"Well, I was thinking that maybe we could make our software faster and more efficient by re-engineering…"

Oh! Finally, you're here. My name is Jacob but people call me Jake. "Okay guys, staff meeting dismissed. Go back to your daily business of coming up with the best ideas in the world!"

I'm delighted you could at last come and enjoy the wonders my company has created for computers, gaming systems and smart phones.

How much money do I make? Well now, that is a difficult question to answer. Considering I designed the first software for my company, Kinetic Software, I usually do make a bit more than my workers here, but mainly, it depends on how many copies of the software we sell. Some years we do well and some years we don't. If we don't do well, I might not make anything!

How did I create this groundbreaking software? Well, when I was growing up, I was always interested in the way things worked. One of my earliest memories was sitting on the kitchen floor with an old phone and attempting to take it apart while my mother cooked me lunch.

My father would come home from his work as a dentist and watch me bang the phone on the floor and study it carefully. Pretty soon I figured out how to take it apart and put it back together. I can remember how excited I had been. I ran around screaming about my accomplishment.

"I got it! I got it, Mommy! I got it, Daddy! I got it, Sissy!" I yelled. My father walked over to me from the other room, scooped me up in his arms and swung me around. He had the broadest smile on his face, as if I had just won Olympic gold.

As I got older, I became interested in science fiction and how the world would work someday. I imagined computers and cell phones and space travel to other planets. I recall my sister, Annabeth, who was about 13, watching TV one day, when I came in, turned the TV off, and told her my latest idea. She called me a twerp, but I didn't care.

"Go bother something else! Don't touch the TV anymore, Jake!" she said in exasperation. With my head hanging low, I walked into my dad's study. He had one of Apple's first computers. When I saw that computer sitting on the dark mahogany desk, I knew what my next project would be. Little did I know that the project of trying to learn how this computer worked would lead to the some of the biggest accomplishments of my life.

It was only a matter of time before I had moved on to developing software to do my part to help change the world! You see, I love what I do, and I live in a country which gives me the freedom to do it. Yes, I work hard, but can you believe I get to make money doing something I love? All you need is passion and freedom – mix a little talent and hard work in there and you'll have something special!

Capitalism Pointer - America's Jobs Come From Capitalism

Adelaide's family came to America to do better through work and the jobs this country had to offer. Jobs come from capitalism. In America, our poorest children have become wealthy adults. Families with no history of higher education have produced doctors and lawyers.

Adelaide and Isabella came from modest beginnings but, as you can see, they've done pretty well. Throughout history, this has not happened in other countries as often as it has in America. It's fairly common in America!

Our country's founders imagined an America with no barriers and no limits on success. Capitalism, with freedom, made it that way. As you read the stories of Adelaide, Isabella, and Jake in this book you'll learn about childhood friends who grow up together.

They will strive to achieve greatness in business and capitalism, helping countless people along the way. Our country has tens of thousands of leaders who are a lot like them. Learning about how our heroes grew up and how they got there will tell us a lot about America and capitalism.

They Said It Long Ago....

Capitalism Helps People - "There is no other way discovered of improving ordinary lives that can get close to the productive activities unleashed by the free-enterprise system."
—Economist Milton Friedman
(paraphrased)

Progress - *"Our great achievements did not come from government... Einstein didn't construct his theory under order from the government. Henry Ford didn't revolutionize the automobile industry that way. The only way for people to escape...poverty...the only cases in recorded history, are where they have had capitalism and free enterprise."*

—*Economist Milton Friedman*
(paraphrased).

We Haven't Found A Better Way - *"Capitalism has worked very well. Anyone who wants to move to North Korea (into government-controlled communism, without freedom) is welcome to do so."*

—*Microsoft Founder Bill Gates.*

5

Adelaide Arrives In America

By the time we arrived in California in the summer of 1973 my parents were already in higher spirits. We quickly gathered our bags and showed our passports once more to a man at the front desk.

"Go ahead," he said to us. I wrapped my hand around the bulky suitcase that contained all my stuff from my life in France and walked towards the glass doors that led to the outside. My parents followed with my baby sister asleep in my mother's arms. The doors slid open and a chilly breeze swept over me, causing me to shiver.

I already miss home, I thought to myself. I felt my father's hand touch my shoulder.

"It's going to be alright, baby doll. Don't worry," he whispered into my ear as we climbed in a yellow taxi cab. I nodded, but questions still flowed through my mind. *Where are we going to live? Is Celeste going to be okay? What if this entire trip is a waste? How are we going to make money? Where am I going to go to school?*

All the questions threatened to spill over my lips, but I didn't want to bother my parents with my worries. I trusted them. I was sure they would have everything figured out. I played with the extra leather on the seat as my father got in the front seat and pulled a small white sheet of paper out of his back pocket.

"Can we please go to 341 Black Blvd, Monterey, California?" my father asked. You see, this sentence made perfect sense to my family and me, but the driver looked confused. The driver murmured something to my father in a language that I did not understand. *Great, this dude doesn't even speak French!* My father sighed heavily and shoved the paper towards the driver.

The driver's green eyes lit up and he nodded towards my father, so I think he understood where we were supposed to be going. I gazed out at the beautiful American landscape that passed as we drove. I assumed California was on the coast because miles and miles of seawater passed to my left side. Sunlight sparkled off the water in magical ways, causing the water to change color. Sometimes it was a deep blue, but when the sun grew brighter, it became a gorgeous green. It was truly magnificent!

My little fantasy was suddenly broken by the high-pitched, annoying sound of Celeste wailing next to me. I smashed my hands over my ears and rested my head on the black door for the rest of the drive, fantasizing about our small apartment in France. There was nowhere else I wanted to be more. I wanted to go home.

My eyes flashed open when I noticed the car came to a screeching stop. The bright sunlight shined through the window, blinding me for a split second. My parents began to exit the taxi cab and I hesitantly followed. *Where are we?* I wondered. My eyes widened as I looked at my surroundings. I was standing about two feet away from a large cliff with a terrifying drop off that led to the beach. Fear gripped my soul as I looked straight down off the ledge. The white sand sparkled, as if the grains of sand were tiny crystals.

I turned away from the tall cliff, fearing I might fall and was shocked by what was behind me. There were two large houses, at least double the size of my small French apartment. They were both at least three stories with gorgeous windows and great architecture.

"Mommy, are those our houses?" I asked, hoping that the answer was yes. Sadly, I did not get my wish.

"No, baby, I'm afraid not. That's our house," she informed me, pointing to a small apartment complex. My heart sunk as I realized we would probably never have enough American money to buy a house like those two. At least that's how it worked in France. I sighed and grabbed my bag from the trunk. I put it on the ground and began walking towards our new home.

My family followed as the man in the taxi cab drove off, brown dust blowing up behind him. When I reached the door, I turned the handle with a shaking hand. The inside was exactly how I had expected it to be—run down, small, with a few pieces of furniture.

"You and your sister will be sharing a room, Ad," my mom told me. I breathed a sigh, and even though I didn't want to do this, this was how it was going to be. This was how it was going to be, from now until I grow up.

"Daddy, where am I going to school?" I asked him, not wanting to know the answer.

He answered calmly and quickly. "You will be going to Garrett Elementary School, just up the road." I opened my mouth to protest, but I stopped myself. And even though I didn't say anything, questions formed in my mind. I wondered how the heck I was supposed to go to school if I couldn't understand a word they said! I trudged to the back room and placed my stuff on one of the two twin beds.

I took a deep breath and looked around, but soon realized there wasn't much to look at. The walls were pure white and the only things in the room were the two twin beds, for me and my sister. I sat down on my bed and put my head in my hands. I knew this trip was going to be hard, but I didn't expect to hate this country so quickly.

6

Isabella Opens Up

I kicked the white sand as hard as I could. I shoved my hands in my pockets and shivered. The strong waves of the Monterey beach crashed against the shore over and over. The sound reminded me of what I wanted to do to all the bullies at my school, Garrett Elementary School. The bright sun and cold breeze was not unfamiliar to me. I started to come to the beach every day for about two weeks now.

I glanced up towards the sun and saw two large houses and a small apartment building on top of the large cliff. Those had not gone unnoticed by my weary eyes either. I envied the people who lived in those two luxurious houses and I was even jealous of the families who could live in the apartments because I knew that whoever lived there probably had friends. I had none.

I sat down on the cold sand and lay on my back, closing my eyes, dreaming of a better life. But I didn't get to stay like that for long. Soon, I heard someone yelling. It was a boy's voice, a voice that was familiar from school. Fear gripped at my stomach as I heard footsteps running down the wooden steps that led to the beach. I closed my eyes once again, hoping that he would just go away.

After all, why would he want to talk to me? *Please let him be alone, and let him leave me alone!* I pleaded to myself, hoping for it with all my heart. Suddenly, the evening sun was blocked by a shadow and I knew that he was standing right above me.

"Hey, you're Isabella Waters right?" he asked me. I was shocked that he even knew my name, but I opened my eyes, there he was, leaning over me. It was none other than Jake Di'Angelo, the most popular and well known boy in the 3rd grade. I sat up and he moved to sit next to me.

"Yeah, how do you know me? Where are your friends?" I questioned him, impatiently waiting for an answer.

"Well, I've seen you around school and you're in my class, but you're always so quiet I thought I should get to know you better. And my friends? Well they would kill me if they knew I was hanging out with you. No offense though." I was shocked by his answer. Jake.... wanted... to... talk... to... me? It took me awhile to process this, but eventually it sunk in.

"How did you get here?" I ask him, expecting him to get up and start laughing with his friends at any moment now.

"Oh, I live right up there," he informed me. He pointed to the big house next to the apartments. I stared, wide-eyed, at the boy sitting in front of me. I had never been this close to him before. I realized his eyes were beautiful hazel instead of brown. I lay back down on the sand, satisfied with the answer, but expecting him to leave.

To my greatest delight, he sat down next to me and we both looked at the setting sun for a brief moment. I found myself actually wanting to talk to him, so I gathered my courage, and asked him the question that's been tugging at my mind since he said hello.

"Why are you here, Jake?" I asked, almost scared of his answer.

"Like I said, you always seem so lonely, and everyone always picks on you, so I thought I would get to know you a little better. You can't be all that bad!" The corners of my mouth turned up in a small smile for the first time in ages. Jake stood up next to me and rolled his sweats up to his knees.

"Ya coming,' Isabella?" he asked me.

"Where?" I wondered aloud.

"Into the shallows of the ocean of course!" he answered me with the swiftest of replies and turned on his heels towards the ocean. I watched as he stepped into the water and yelled as the freezing water touched his skin. I weighed my choices for a moment. Should I go have fun with the popular boy and get soaking wet or should I stay here and be friendless for the rest of my life?

I knew the answer immediately. I rolled up the bottom of my ripped jeans and dashed after him into the water. I shrieked as my feet made contact with the ice cold ocean. Suddenly, I felt something icy splash me in the face, drenching my hair. I screamed in surprise and when I opened my eyes, I saw Jake snickering behind his hands.

"Ohhh, I will get you, Jake Di'Angelo!" I yelled, chasing after him. I threw my head back and laughed as I drenched him with sea water. I realized for the first time since my father's death, I was…. happy. For the first time since my father's death, I had smiled, laughed, and began to trust someone. Who would have ever guessed that Jake Di'Angelo would become my first real friend?

7

Jake Cares And Begins To Lead The Way

I walked into my house, drenched from head to toe, but I didn't care. Today, I met a friend, Isabella. Not a fake friend, like all my guy friends who hang out with me just because of sports, but an actual friend. Someone I can trust with my secrets, my fears, my worries. At least that's what I'm hoping will happen.

"Jake! What happened to you? You're getting the mat all wet!" my sister screamed, running up the steps to grab a towel. When she returned, she was holding a fluffy yellow bath towel. She shoved it in my face and I took it, drying myself off.

"By the way Jake, we're going over to visit the new neighbors from France tonight. Look presentable, brush your hair!" she ordered me.

I had always hated when Annabeth gave me orders. My parents were on a business trip, so Annabeth, being 19 now, was in charge. "Brush your hair, Jake! Look presentable, Jake!"

I mocked. "I look fine, AB. Let's go now." She sighed, but nodded her thin head, causing her long auburn hair to swing.

"Go put on dry clothes first," she ordered again. I groaned and trudged up the steps to my room. My sister grabbed a plate of cookies to give to the new people and after I changed and put on dry tennis shoes, we walked out the front door towards the new neighbors.

"Now, Jake, these people might be a little different than us, so we have to be respectful," my sister reminded me.

I had heard this many times before. "I know," I replied. The stars in the black night sky twinkled like diamonds as we knocked on their wooden door. I was expecting something different, but I was not prepared for what their family was like. A tall woman with a crying toddler in her arms answered the door, looking stressed and tired.

"Hello, sorry to interrupt, but we're your next door neighbors, we heard you were new to our country, and we just wanted to introduce our family to yours. I am Annabeth and this is my brother, Jake," she said, extending her hand towards the woman. The woman looked confused and frazzled. She said something loud and clear in a language I didn't understand.

"No English?"" My sister asked them, biting her lower lip. The inside of their house appeared empty and quiet, as if no one was living there at all. The woman still looked confused. Suddenly, I saw a girl about my age, with long blonde hair and large blue eyes enter the empty room. She walked confidently up to me and extended her hand to me. Her mother whispered something to her in their language, a warning maybe? But the girl ignored her.

"I'm Adelaide," the girl informed me with a heavy French accent. I took her hand and shook it, shocked that she understood something.

"Jake, nice to meet you?" I questioned her, wondering if she understood a word I just said. She flashed a white smile towards me, so I assumed she understood. I took the white ceramic plate from my sister and handed her the chocolate chip cookies. Her blue eyes lit up with excitement.

"Merci!" she told me. At first I didn't understand, but I finally got the hint that she just said thank you.

"Thank you?" I confirmed. She nodded her head slowly and smiled lightly. I waved goodbye to Adelaide.

"Au revoir!" she told me when she had made sense of my parting wave.

"Goodbye, Adelaide," I translated. I closed the door and turned to my sister, who stood next to me, unmoving.

"Where the heck did you learn that, Jake?" she asked, completely stunned. I just smiled, satisfied with myself, and began to walk home in the dark. Annabeth followed slowly, in some sort of trance and my thoughts returned to Isabella from earlier today. I wondered if together, we could somehow teach English to Adelaide. Would she let us? What would happen if we succeeded? Little did I know at the time this would be one of the greatest journeys of my life.

Capitalism Pointer – High Morals Can Help Capitalism, Businesses and Jobs

You can already begin to see that Jake has a great shot at growing up with high morals. He wants to help people. What do high morals have to do with capitalism, businesses and jobs? Quite a lot! Our relationships in life depend on how we treat one another. Are we honest? Do we respect other people and their property? Are we violent or peaceful? Do we steal? Do we give our best effort? Do we treat one another well? Our faith and our morals can make all the difference.

Think of it this way. Our business and work relationships are just like other relationships in life. They thrive and succeed with honesty, trust and respect for others. If you entered into a business partnership with another person, or if you placed your faith in a new employee, you would expect these things. Freedom and capitalism work better when people do right by one another.

On the other hand, relationships, including work relationships, usually fail when people have low morals. Failed relationships cost businesses money and they cause businesses to lose out on opportunities. *Businesses without ethics often hurt people and, in a way, they hurt capitalism.*

A team of hard working people who respect one another can accomplish almost anything in business. They can literally change lives. If you have Jake's approach to life, and if you work hard, you will have a great chance to succeed.

They Said It Long Ago...

Freedom Has Responsibilities - "*Our United States constitution was made for a moral people. Our country with freedom and democracy won't work if we become an immoral people.*"

—President John Adams
(paraphrased)

8

Friends For Life?

Poverty- the state of being extremely poor. Well, I guess that pretty much describes my family right now. I closed the French translation dictionary and sat it on the small new wooden table next to me with a sigh. Celeste was home from her first treatment in America. It has only been three months since we moved here and my parents have both gotten jobs working at a large factory not too far from our apartment.

Our living room just had a small dark wood table and a beat up couch, but it was an improvement. My bedroom had sheets and a few blankets over the beds while my parents put up wallpaper in their room. Tomorrow is my first day of school and the thought of it made my stomach churn. I now know some of the basic words of English.

Most of this language was even easier than French, but some words I studied tricked me and I can't seem to figure them out. I felt a chilly breeze whoosh through the crack under the broken window pane, causing me to shudder. I grabbed a jacket from my bag and slung it quickly over my shoulders, hugging it close. *I need to get out of this place.* I thought, itching to escape the blank walls of my hut that were threatening to suffocate me if I stayed any longer.

"Mom, I'm going out to the beach," I shouted to her. She didn't answer, so I suspected it was fine. I walked out the front door, zipping up my light jacket. The powerful California wind sent my blonde hair streaming behind me. When I reached the cliff to the beach, I looked around for a moment before finally spotting a wooden staircase that led to the ocean.

As I walked down, I heard a gorgeous sound that I had not heard since I left France. It was.....laughter. The sound was coming from a girl with curly brown locks and a boy with spiked black hair. The boy chased the girl around the beach, causing her to squeal and shriek with delight. I sighed and turned to walk away, not wanting to interrupt, but then I heard someone call my name.

"Adelaide!" the boy shouted. I whipped my head around, pushing my hair out of my eyes. I squinted my blue eyes to get a closer look at the boy. I stifled a gasp as I recognized Jake, the boy who had come to give my family cookies on our first night. I gave him a small smile and waved slightly. The girl that he was with stopped running and turned to look at me in confusion. She asked him something, but the sound was drowned out by the fierce wind.

He raised his hand and motioned for me to come down on the beach. I hesitated, wondering if this was the best idea, but then I decided that this experience might be good for me. I slowly stepped down the steps, wincing every time they creaked. When I reached the wet sand, I hesitantly approached the two kids.

"Hello," I whispered, my thick French accent practically butchering the simple word.

"Hey, Adelaide." Jake said. "This is Isabella." he informed me, pointing to the girl. I gave her a small smile and shook her extended hand. Isabella, not realizing that I didn't completely understand what she was saying, asked me a question. The only words I caught were "do," "you," "want," "to," "with," and "us." I looked at her confused as Jake whispered something in her ear and her mouth opened in an understanding "O."

Jake repeated the word that I didn't catch in that sentence.

"Play," he told me, poking Isabella in the stomach, and began to run. She ran after him, laughter hanging suspended in the air as she ran. Eventually, she poked him in the back and stopped, sticking her tongue out at him. Jake looked defeated as he trudged over to me. "Play," he repeated. "Do you want to play with us?" My eyes widened in appreciation and I nodded anxiously.

"You're it!" Isabella yelled. I really didn't get the meaning of that, but she began to run from Jake, so I ran too. Eventually, I picked up on the game. I was supposed to run from the person who was "it" and then if I was tagged, then I was "it" and had to tag other people.

When night fell, I returned to the house, laughing and smiling more than ever. I found out they were also attending Garrett Elementary School, so maybe the following day would be bearable with them by my side.

For the next year, we each came to the beach and chatted, played, and did homework. It wasn't long before we grew very close. They'd spend hours with me every day, teaching me more and more English.

After our fourth month of this, I was almost fluent in the English language, causing me to be the first in my family to accomplish this—but that was just the beginning. Over time, I would be the first of my family to do a lot of things. America wasn't so bad after all.

Capitalism Pointer – Much of Our Hope Can Come From Capitalism

Adelaide is just really beginning to hope for a better tomorrow. Hope is such an important part of our lives. Success doesn't happen overnight. Why do we go to more school after high school? Why do we need to do good work at our jobs? Because we hope to make a better life for ourselves and our families!

When we see people building successful businesses through capitalism, it helps us see how we can improve our chances of success. We have hope. If they can do it, there's no reason we can't do it even better!

With capitalism, people can find new, better jobs they didn't have before. Jake, Adelaide and Isabella will be a big part of this as they grow older. One really successful business can help improve thousands of lives. As we hope for better jobs and better opportunities for our families, there's no doubt that a lot of our hope comes from capitalism, even if we don't usually think of it that way.

With capitalism, and in life, one success can also lead to another success. Doing a good job today may lead to a better job tomorrow. The employees of businesses today may have their own businesses tomorrow. Their children may go into business. They've seen success and how it works. They know how work builds confidence and self-esteem. Money has been earned and lives have been changed. Now, with all of these people starting businesses, tens of thousands of lives of families can be improved.

Thousands of businesses can improve millions of lives. When we're successful in doing this across the country, every person who wants a good job has an opportunity to earn one. Everyone who works hard and smart has the money needed for their families.

What is the best hope for a family? One of their best hopes is when a family member gets a great job. As you earn more money, your family usually has a better chance of doing well. Students often do better and learn more when they live in a home which is doing well. Hope can come from many things in life. One of those things is a great job and the chance for an even better one – which can come from capitalism.

All of this is just common sense and there's nothing complicated about it. But for capitalism to work, we need to understand it and believe in ourselves. As you continue reading this book, we hope you view our country and capitalism in a different, better way.

We hope you begin to see our country's great accomplishments, many of which came to us because of capitalism! Jake, Adelaide, and Isabella may stumble and fall at times, but they figure it out. So will you!

They Said It Long Ago...

Everyone Has Purpose And Opportunity - Every individual life is infinitely precious, that every one of us put in this world has been put there for a reason and has something to offer. It's impossible for government to substitute for millions of individuals working night and day to make their dreams come true!"

—President Ronald Reagan

The Land of Hope - "Never forget that this is America, the land where dreams come true."

—President Ronald Reagan

9

Growing Pains for Isabella

As time passed, Adelaide began to grow on me, but there were definitely things I wish I could change about her. I love Adelaide; don't get me wrong, but sometimes…she can be a bit…what's the word? Clingy? The only reason I'm saying this is because Jake seems to like hanging out with her better than he does hanging out with me.

She follows him around in school like a little lost puppy, which I know she no longer is. It's been several years now since we started spending time together and everyone in our trio is thirteen.

For the past few months, Jake always seems to laugh more when I'm not there. When I sit somewhere else at lunch, he smiles more. You can practically see the excitement in his eyes when I'm not there. I've seen them at the beach many times when I couldn't come with them, laughing, talking, and smiling. He's thrown me away like an old, worn out sweater. The last time we talked was about two weeks ago.

We used to be inseparable, talking and seeing each other every day, but not anymore. What happened to those golden days? What thing stepped in between the two of us and stole his attention with her huge blue eyes and full blonde hair. Oh, that's right, Adelaide. Perfect, beautiful, Adelaide.

Honestly, when I met her, I never imagined she would grow up to be this pretty, but she has, and Jake seems to have noticed. Her French accent seems to draw everyone in, making them want to listen, keeping them there until they are hypnotized by her beauty and never want to leave her side.

Let's face it; Adelaide is the most popular girl at school now. She may not have the biggest house, or the best clothes, but nevertheless, everyone seems to love her anyway. Even now, as I sit on the opposite side of the cafeteria, trying to avoid eye contact with anyone else, Jake and Addie are surrounded by other 7th graders.

Occasionally, I would hear Jake's distinct voice, or the beautiful ring of Adelaide's laughter. Whenever this happened, I would continue to stare at my uneaten food, wanting to go over there and join in, but not having enough courage. I never had enough courage. I picked up my plastic fork and attempted to eat something, with no luck. My appetite was nowhere to be found.

"Yeah, I know, guys! I can't ever imagine living without you!" Adelaide yelled to the group surrounding her. That struck a chord. She had said the same exact thing to me a year ago, but look at me now! Someone had to push her off her pedestal of ego and that person would be me. I jumped up, slamming my chair back into the table as I pushed it in, and stalked over to her. I quickly tapped her on the shoulder before I lost my adrenaline.

"Do you remember when you said the same thing to me, Addie?" I asked her. She flinched at the sound of her old nickname and turned around to face me.

"Oh, Isabella! Where have you been? I miss you so much!" she announced loudly, making sure everyone heard it. She held her arms open wide and tried to wrap me in a hug. I pushed her away with a hard shove.

"I'm surprised you even remember my name with all your new friends and such!" I yelled, glancing at everyone surrounding Jake and Adelaide. "And what about you, huh?" I asked, pointing at Jake. "What happened to hanging out with ole' Bella?"

Jake stood up and held his arms up, as if surrendering to something. "Look, Isabella, I didn't mean to be ignoring you, but things have just been so hectic lately and...," he started.

"No, I don't want your filthy apologies. You haven't said a word to me in the past two weeks, and you've spent all your waking hours with your new best friend! What happened to the three of us being friends forever?" I asked him, holding back tears from spilling down my cheeks in front of the entire seventh grade. But I knew I couldn't hold them back for much longer, so I ran out without another word, leaving the queen bee with her mouth hanging open in surprise.

10

Jake Mends Fences

Guilt, shame, humiliation, mortification, indignity, I felt all of these things, but most of all, I felt sorry. I felt horrible, like I had just witnessed someone get murdered and did nothing to stop it. My heart twisted and wrenched for Isabella. Had we been ignoring her? Now that I think of it, we had, but not intentionally! I would never do that to her.

She was my first real friend and even though it was almost six years ago, I will never forget that day. She means something to me, and if somebody means something to you, they never truly stop meaning something to you. Once they mean something, they'll never just be "another person" to you again. That's what it's like with me and Isabella.

Sure, Adelaide means a lot to me, too, but we will never have the same bond Isabella and I have. I looked over at Adelaide sitting next to me. She was staring at the ground, not blinking, perfect pink lips in a wide "O" shape. I put a hand on her shoulder and her head snapped up to me, as if she was just snapped out of a trance.

"Do you want to go talk to her?" I asked, noticing the crowd that always surrounds our lunch tables had quickly dwindled to just a few awkward bystanders.

"No, I really don't think she wants to talk to the girl who stole her best friend right now. You go talk to her alone," Adelaide told me. It was not a suggestion. It was an order. I patted her shoulder awkwardly with my hand and got up to follow Isabella. I caught a glimpse of her brown hair streaming out the cafeteria door and broke into a sprint to catch up with her.

"Isabella!" I called out to her, ignoring the judgmental stares I received from people. We ran through the hallway with me at her heels. Just as she was about to turn into the girl's bathroom, I caught her arm in my grasp. She struggled for a bit.

"Let go of me, Jake!" she yelled, pulling and tugging on her arm.

"No, not until you listen. Now let's make this painless. Stop struggling so we can talk," I told her. She slumped to the hallway floor and sat there, waiting expectantly for my explanation. I sat down next to her.

"Listen, Bella, we didn't mean to ignore you. I would never do that to you on purpose. You're practically my sister. I wouldn't hurt you like that. I've known you for six years and have I ever done that to you?" I asked, almost afraid of her answer.

"No….," she whispered, seeming defeated already.

"That's what I thought. Now listen to me when I say that you are so special to me. I would be so lost without my best friend. We're a trio, not a pair and I plan on it staying like that."

"But you guys are so popular and I'm such a loser. I just don't fit in with you anymore, Jake," she whimpered, causing my heart to sink.

"No, that's not true at all. You're not a loser. You never have been and you never will be, at least in my book that is," I paused for a second and then continued, "and if you do end up being a loser, Adelaide and I will become losers with you!"

The smile on her face caused my heart to soar into the sky as she hugged me. "Thank you, Jake, for everything," she whispered in my ear. We got up from the floor and walked back to the cafeteria where we're found Adelaide pacing nervously. Everyone kept their distance from her, as if they were afraid they too, would be ignored if they go to close. When she saw us, she ran up to Isabella and threw her arms around her.

"I'm sorry. So sorry," I heard her say.

"Its fine… Addie," Isabella whispered. I saw the corners of Adelaide's mouth turn up in a smile as she heard her nickname being used once again. Let's just say the three of us never got into a fight again. It was smooth seas ahead for our trio.

Part Two
A Path to Success with Advanced Learning

11

Adelaide Looks To The Future With Anxiety

High school. I'll be a graduate of the Class of 1984. This stuff is an entirely different world than middle school. Honestly, I'm really proud I made it this far in life. I made it through all of middle school and three years of high school with A's and B's, but senior year is hard! Much harder than I expected it would be and I don't know how well I will do. I hope I can keep up my grades, but I will have to focus a lot more than I did the years before.

Keeping up my average is very important now that I am just one short year away from college... that is, if I can find the money to go to college. My sister just had her last surgery about three months ago and she's improving, but it's hard to save enough money for college. Luckily, my father has been climbing up the business ladder at the local power plant and he comes home every year with a raise. But even with the raises and bonuses, I will still have to get a scholarship of some sort, or work during school, to pay the ginormous college fees.

What will I major in and study in college, you may ask? I have no idea yet. Jake has already decided he will go into technology and engineering. Isabella is thinking about going into business, but me? I don't really know. I guess I'll just have to wait to find out. I haven't even been accepted to college yet.

"Ms. Adelaide, can you answer the question written on the board?" Mrs. Ferrin, my senior math teacher, asked me. *Dang it, I zoned out again!* I mentally scolded myself as I looked at the calculus problem written on the board for everybody to see and solve.

"Umm, I'm a little confused, Mrs. Ferrin. Can you help me?" I asked sweetly, thickening my French accent to add the effect of innocence and pleasantness. A smile formed on my teacher's pale face.

"Why of course I can, sweetie," she cooed as she began to explain how to answer the problem. Luckily, this was my last period of the day and there was only three minutes of class left, so before she got to finish, the bell rang and all the students piled out of the door.

On my way to my locker, I caught up to Jake and Isabella. I saw their intertwined hands and smiled to myself. Let's just say that, over time, something had finally sparked between the two of them and it wasn't long before Jake finally asked her out on the last day of junior year.

"How was sixth period?" Isabella asked me.

"Horrible, I can't wait to go to Frozen Berry." I told them, referring to our high school tradition of going to the local ice cream place, Frozen Berry, after school every Friday.

"Neither can I. I have some exciting news to tell you guys," Jake told us. He had that excited, yet sneaky look in his eyes. As we exited the school, Bella and I begged Jake to tell us his news, but he refused to budge. We all piled into Jake's fancy silver Volvo.

He was the only one of our trio who got a car for his sixteenth birthday and I think I speak for Isabella, too, when I say we're jealous of his car. It's sleek and shiny and not too big. Once again, I find myself wanting to be successful enough someday to buy a car like that. Who knows, maybe I will be someday.

But I pushed the thought away from my mind as we pulled into the parking lot of Frozen Berry.

The three of us walked into the colorful store and ordered our usual flavors. Mine was pomegranate. Isabella's was plain vanilla and Jake's was Boston Cheesecake. We sat down at one of the small wooden booths and waited anxiously for Jake to spill.

"Okay…. Ready?" he asked, teasing us. We nodded impatiently. "Jake Di'Angelo will be attending the University of California! I got my acceptance letter last night and I have half scholarship!" Isabella and I shrieked with excitement, causing people to stare at us.

"Oh my gosh, Jake, that's amazing!" Isabella thrilled, getting up to hug him. When she let go, a smile had formed on her face, her eyes glinting with excitement.

"And, now, I have some news of my own!" she told us, sitting back down next to me.

"What is it?" I asked.

"Isabella Waters will be attending…. Yale University with a full scholarship!" she yelled. I stared at her wide eyed. I knew that she was a straight A student, but a full scholarship to one of the best schools in the country? I was happy, but I couldn't stop myself from feeling a bit envious of the two. As they hugged and talked about how amazing college life would be I sat there without a scholarship, without an acceptance letter, but with one question racking my brain. What college would I get into?

12

Isabella Looks To The Future With Confidence

Yes, that's right guys. I will be attending Yale University! It took a lot of hard work and hours and hours of putting together an Ivy League resumé, but it all paid off in the long run. It was definitely one the best moments of my life when I opened the acceptance letter. And I'm even happier for Jake! University of California is awesome for him... But I will admit that I'm going to miss him. Of course, right as we hit it off, life leads us down separate paths.

We could always try a long distance relationship, but to tell you the truth, I don't think that I could handle that. I mean, with all my studies at Yale, it would just be too much for me to handle. But that's not the issue right now because we still have six months until college. The issue right now is getting Adelaide into college. Twenty-four weeks until our first day and still nothing from any college? That is just unacceptable! She is a bright and beautiful girl and any college would be lucky to have her!

I'm sure she will get into something, but I could tell from her expression at Frozen Berry she was worried. Worried about the college she would get into - or if she would even get in at all. Suddenly, my train of thought was broken by the sharp trill of my phone. I picked it up.

"Hello," I said.

"Hey, Isabella! Come over to my house right now! I have some big news!!" It was Adelaide's voice on the other end.

"Okay, I will be right over!" I told her, grabbing my purse and sprinting out the door without hesitation. What happened? Is Jake already there? She sounded excited, which is a good sign! Did she get accepted into a college? Oh, I sure hope that's what has gotten her so enthusiastic. I started my car and drove quickly to her small house. When I got there, I jumped out of the car and knocked on their door. Adelaide's mother answered with a big smile on her face.

"Oh, hello, Isabella! Adelaide is in her room," her mom said, her French accent making it a bit hard to understand. I practically shoved past her and raced into Adelaide's room where she and Jake were sitting on Adelaide's bed. Celeste, now a smaller replica of her sister, was sitting on the other bed with a sneaky smile.

"You might want to sit down, Bella. This news is a little tough to process." Jake said, grabbing my shoulders and leading me to sit on Celeste's bed. Adelaide took a deep breath and began.

"Well, I know it might be shocking, but..... I got into the University of California with Jake! We get to go to the same college!" she shrieked, jumping and clapping like a little kid.

"Isn't that amazing, Isabella?" Jake yelled, joining her in the celebration.

"Yeah, that's awesome!" I agreed, putting all my fake enthusiasm into the party. Sure, it was great they would both be going to the same school, but Jake is my boyfriend and I can't help but feel resentful of Adelaide. She will get to spend an extra four to seven years with him while I am halfway across the country! I have confidence I will do well at Yale, but I'm also confident I will miss Jake.

13

Jake Looks To The Future With Nervous Anticipation

Well, this is it. Several months have passed since the day Adelaide and I announced that we were attending the same college and graduation day has finally rolled around. And guess what? My best friend, Isabella Waters, is this year's class valedictorian! I'm so excited for college and for high school to end, but I am going to miss her. By her, I mean Bella. We are still together, and I'm all for a long distance relationship, but she seems to think that we're not worth it anymore...

But I can't worry about that right now. I need to put on that hat and robe and get out onto stage. I grabbed my hat and stuffed it onto my head, covering up my spiked black hair. Then, I grabbed the blue robe and slowly put my arms into it, pulling it over my shoulders.

Where is Adelaide? I thought, spying Isabella talking to the principal. Eventually, I spotted Adelaide's long blonde hair through the crowd and pushed my way through.

"Excuse me. Sorry, pardon me," I murmured as I bumped into multiple students, receiving death glares from my fellow graduates.

"Guess who?" I whispered in Adelaide's ear, covering my hands over her eyes.

"Ummm, Jake?" she questioned, giggling.

"You got it! Now, c'mon, let's go get our diplomas!!" I told her, stepping ahead of her and walking into the wings of the stage.

"Thank you everyone for attending this year's graduation. Now, I would like to introduce our very important people tonight. Ladies and gentleman please give a warm welcome to the Riverview High graduation class of 1984!" Principal Grendewald's announcement caused a roar of clapping from our friends and families in the audience as we walked onto the stage. As the class filed into the stage, Isabella stepped up to the microphone as class valedictorian.

"Well hello, everybody. Thank you for coming. I am really proud...," she started. While Isabella spoke, my mind began to wander during the remainder of her speech. As time passed, the excitement of graduating dwindled into a giant wave of stress that threatened to crash over my head. What would college life be like? What if I failed my classes and never made it through college? What if it college life is not all it cracked up to be?

I could go through a thousand what if's that were racing through my mind, but soon, I heard the crowd applaud loudly, signaling the end of Isabella's speech. *This is it. High school is over. I'm getting my diploma*, I thought.

Beads of sweat began to form on my forehead as Mrs. Grendewald started calling names. I quickly wiped my forehead as I realized my name was only a few away. My heart began to race and pound inside my chest. I gulped and took one deep breath to calm the butterflies that fluttered around in my stomach.

"Jake Di'Angelo," Mrs. Grendewald announced. My heart felt like it was going to explode out of my chest. I stared at my feet as I made my way up to my principal. My head was spinning so fast that I worried it might just possibly fall right off my head! I extended my hand out to my principal to grab the diploma and my eyes met her. She gave me a comforting flash of her pearly white teeth and handed the white roll of paper to me.

In a trance, I walked back and stood next to Adelaide, who anxiously awaited the announcement of her name. Some of my nerves began to ease as I heard Adelaide's name boomed through the speaker. They had gone completely when Mrs. Grendewald called Isabella's name near the end.

"Now, please move your tassels from the right to the left," the principal stated. Everyone obliged, moving the golden tassels to the opposite side of their caps with large beaming smiles on their faces.

"Congratulations, everyone, you have officially graduated!" she announced. All the graduate seniors responded by throwing their blue hats as high as they can towards the ceiling. Yes, I finally graduated high school and this part of my life was over, but I felt like my life was just beginning. Whatever happens, it will be a wild ride, I'm sure.

Capitalism Pointer - Capitalism Helps All of Us

Adelaide, Jake and Isabella are about to start a true American journey. In America we usually succeed through hard work and overcoming obstacles in our path. Business leaders and their great employees are often excellent examples of this. They can teach us to toughen up, plan, and sacrifice because big successes can occur, but they rarely occur overnight. This is how life and business usually work. You can see how Adelaide, Jake and Isabella have prepared to get a great start.

When we have to work for something, it means a lot. When we risk everything we own to get there, like business owners often do, it can mean even more. Capitalism is, as they say, "as American as apple pie." Every time a business person succeeds, it reminds us that we can get there too. Americans weren't created to stand still or settle for second best.

Capitalism encourages us, whether we like it or not, to strive to get better. We seek more education to improve our chance of success. We learn things and get smarter. We work smart to find a way to earn more. As we work, we learn things we never knew. A surprising thing happens along the way. We can usually become happier in our lives.

We might have successes and failures, but when capitalism works, we end up with the job we are meant to do or the business we are meant to run. Again, a surprising thing happens. Through the struggle, we can become even happier in our lives.

Capitalism is not an easy path, but if it were easy, we wouldn't learn much or get stronger. How do you think we invented things like airplanes and telephones? The money from capitalism in our country built amazing skyscraper, airports, roads and bridges. These things weren't easy. We invented and built them with American spirit and capitalism.

There's something big at the end of the rainbow with American spirit and capitalism. When we find our way, through struggles and hardship, with education and hard work, we can handle life's challenges. The things we learn in life and on the job help us to become better communicators, better parents and better friends. We make progress and grow in life.

We develop confidence and skills to help others. We understand life better. We don't get this good by letting others do the work for us. Capitalism is part of the American experience which tells us that if we strive to be the best we can be, life can be better than we ever imagined.

They Said It Long Ago...

One Country - "Let us not seek the Republican answer or the Democratic answer, but the right answer. Let us not seek to fix the blame for the past. Let us accept our own responsibility for our American future."

—President John F. Kennedy

Solutions, Not Problems – "We in government should learn to look at our country with the eyes of the business person, seeing possibilities where others see only problems."

—President Ronald Reagan

14

Adelaide Goes To College With A Sense of Adventure

I loaded my last bag into the trunk of Jake's Volvo with a grunt as I lifted the heavy pink tote. The cheerful late summer sun beat down onto my tan skin, making it shimmer and shine in the light. The scent of roses filled my nose as I watched Jake hand a beautiful bouquet of red roses to Isabella. They decided it was best for them to go their separate ways during college, but if they somehow ended up meeting again someday then it might be meant to be.

"I'm going to miss you guys so much," Isabella gushed, leaving Jake and hugging me tightly. Today, Jake and I were off to college at the University of California and tomorrow, Isabella would be traveling all the way to Yale. Our first day of college was in less than two weeks and, despite leaving Isabella, Jake and I were ecstatic for the college life.

"I'm going to miss you, too, Bella," I whispered, squeezing her small figure. Traitor tears threatened to spill down my cheeks as I let her go and climbed into the passenger's side of the car. I waved to my waiting parents from inside and gave them a small smile. Needless to say, they were proud of me. I was the first person in the history of my family to ever graduate high school and attend college.

My family promised to send me a small allowance to help me along, but paying for lots of school would be up to me. They waved back at me, my sister, an excited wave, my mother and father, a heart wrenching wave with tears rolling down their cheeks. They were really going to miss me, and I was definitely going to miss them.

We had been through so much together. We came to America together, survived my sister's hard times together, and made a life together. I had always been a very independent girl, but every child needs their parents once in a while. I stole one last glance at my family, Jake's family, and Isabella real quick before Jake stepped on the pedal and the car lurched forward.

"College life, here we come!" Jake shouted, rolling down the windows and turning up the radio. Wind ripped through my hair, blowing it far behind me and at that moment, I felt free. With the wind rushing on my face and the sun sparkling in my eyes, I felt like I could rise to dramatic heights and do amazing things for my family. I felt like I could do ANYTHING.

Capitalism Pointer - Education Is A Key To Capitalism

You can see how excited Jake and Adelaide are about going off to college. They should be! Smart businesses are also excited for them! Whether students attend community college, trade school, or go to a university, businesses need educated, intelligent people. These people usually become their best employees. Without education, people would rarely be able to develop the knowledge and skills to do great work. The bottom line is that without education, capitalism and businesses cannot succeed!

As you learn about capitalism, remember, all of the pieces of a puzzle must fit together for a country to work. We need good government, great education, and strong businesses. In some ways, we all look out for one another, and we all look out for the country.

15

Isabella Has To Work For College Success

There they went, smiles plastered on their faces, heads thrown back in laughter. I'll never forget it. And here I sit, my second semester at Yale, at my desk, coming up on my fifth hour of homework. My two best friends are probably having the time of their lives over at their university, getting a good education, but at the same time, having fun and making friends.

Okay, now I'm not knocking any of the students at Yale here, because I'm sure they will all grow up to become amazing multi-millionaires or politicians, but the students here are NOT very entertaining. All they talk about is science, math and philosophy. They rarely go out and have fun, and almost never have parties, which I'm told should be one of the best college experiences. Most of what I do is study, study, study.

I thought college was about making memories, not spending all your hours studying and doing work. I have made exactly zero friends so far here at the university. I am smart, yes. I do understand the lessons, yes, but I'm not as smart as many of them. I have to work at it. I feel suffocated in this world of brainiacs and professors. I have come to the conclusion that with good schooling and a steady job, you can do or be anything you want. I'll do whatever it takes.

This is why I have decided I will push through these years of my life at Yale and have fun later in life because there is always a time to have fun and a time to work. Now is the time to work. In the years to come, I plan to move to a new state with Adelaide and Jake and actually start my life.

Suddenly, I heard my phone ring on the light mahogany desk that has become my home for the past six months. It was Jake!

"How is life with your smarty friends?" Jake quipped. A smile broke from my face. His comments always made me smile when I was feeling under the weather.

"It stinks. I miss you guys! When can we meet up?" I quickly replied, hoping that it was soon.

"Ummm… What are you doing three weekends from now?" I could hear the hopefulness in his voice, so I thought for a second, praying that I was free. I pulled out my plain black calendar (which was all I could afford on the low budget that I live off of now) and checked the date. I was free! Yes, freedom!

"I'm free. Where do you wanna meet?" I asked. I could practically feel the freedom already. I had hoped we could see each other in California. I want to smell the salty tang of the sea, and feel the cold California breeze. I needed to go home!

"I was thinking we could go back to the beach where we first met, where the three of us became friends," he said. My heart leapt with joy and I quickly replied saying that I would love that.

I can imagine it right now. The freezing salt water running over my bare legs, getting in my hair, the wind ripping at my skin, freezing it in the cold winter breeze, but I didn't care. I could practically picture it now, and it was perfect, beautifully, blissfully, perfect.

Capitalism Pointer - Great Education Comes From Capitalism and Businesses

Adelaide, Jake and Isabella decided to go to college to increase their chances of success. Education, most of which comes from government, is no doubt one of the most important things in life. Some people say that all they really care about is education.

But without capitalism, education wouldn't be very good, and it wouldn't be nearly as useful. Here's why. Taxes paid by businesses and their employees provide the money for schools. If capitalism fails or struggles, we have fewer businesses, fewer employees, and fewer tax dollars. It's pretty hard to have great teachers and great schools when that happens.

It's not just about tax dollars from businesses and their employees. If a family doesn't have a good job, it can be tougher for their children to focus on getting a great education. Everybody wins with strong capitalism, businesses and jobs, including education!

But there's something which feels even worse about education when capitalism is not working well. Many people do go to college to get a great job. What if they get out of college and there are no jobs? Imagine being one of the most educated people around, without a good job. With healthy capitalism and businesses, this will almost never happen.

Anybody who wants great cities, great education, and great jobs for students should root for businesses and capitalism, shouldn't they? Maybe you can help more people see this part of how the country works. The truth is that when capitalism and businesses do well, America does well.

16

Reunited

Wet sand squished under my Nike tennis shoes as I wrapped my arms around my chest in an attempt to keep warm.

"Where is she?" Adelaide protested, clearly just as uncomfortable with the cold as I was.

"I'm sure her plane was just a little late. She will be here soon.... I know it," I replied, mainly trying to reassure myself. Isabella hates being late. She always has and now she was almost an entire hour late. It had been three weeks since we had arranged this meeting and I'm beginning to worry about her. Wind tore at my jacket, stinging my skin.

Suddenly, I heard footsteps sprint down the creaky staircase from the hill. Then I saw a whoosh of brown hair and a glimpse of brown eyes. The pair of us on the beach ran towards the bottom of the staircase, impatiently awaiting Isabella's arrival.

When she finally got to us, there was a lot of squealing from the girls as they shared a hug. I admit I joined in. When we untangled ourselves I could finally see Isabella's face. Her eyes looked tired and worn out, but full of life.

It's like she has just awoke from the dead and has been reunited with her family. Which in a way, she has. We are family. We have been, and I hope we always will be. Hand in hand, we walked towards a rock at the edge of the water and jumped on top of it.

"When did this rock start to shrink?" Isabella laughed, squeezing herself next to me.

"When did we get so big?" Adelaide teased, giggling.

"Okay, so tell me, guys. How is life at the University of California?" Isabella asked, leaning forward as if about to hear some big gossip.

"Isabella, we have nice, heated dorms with a library and a lounge and a bunch of picnic tables to eat outside, if you remember to bring a jacket! And the best part is there are a lot of cool people. Everyone seems pretty chill, but focused at the same time!" Honestly, I could have gone on and on, but I decided to spare Isabella my rant.

"That sounds amazing, guys. I wish I could be there with you," she trailed off, a look of longing in her deep brown eyes, but as quick as she left, she was back. "So tell me, are you guys thinking about staying in California when you get older?"

I had to think for a moment. Sure, I love the cool breezes, the wet beaches, and the spring rains, but do I really want to stay here forever?

"I don't know, Bella. I was thinking about going to New York and opening my own clothing line," Adelaide replied. She had always loved the idea of fashion even though she could never afford designer clothes as a kid, nor can she buy them now. She loved the bright colors and the expressive ways of having your own style, so naturally, it had always been her dream to be a designer, but we never imagined she'd actually follow through on it.

"Oh, would I get a discount on your clothes?" Isabella asked, half teasing. "What about you, Jake? Where do you want to live"

"Ummm, I'm not sure, maybe here or maybe somewhere else. I haven't really put that much thought into it yet," I replied. Suddenly, I felt icy rain drops land on my forehead, making me shiver. The rain quickly picked up into an unsympathetic downpour, drenching us within seconds. Adelaide let out a scream and covered her perfect blonde hair with her hands.

"C'mon, let's go into my house!" I yelled, making a break for the steps up the rocky hill. The girls were hot at my heels, Adelaide screeching like a banshee, as if she were actually going to melt. Isabella ran quietly, laughing softly, but just loud enough to be heard over the pounding drops falling on the blacktop roads. *She still loves the rain,* I thought to myself, smiling as I realized she's still the same girl that I have always known.

Once I reached my front door, I pounded on the wood, ringing the doorbell frantically with my free hand. My mom opened the door, looking startled and frazzled at the sight of three old friends – now three drenched college students.

"Hi, guys. Come inside and dry off," she said. The two shivering icicles nodded quickly, rushing in the front door. I followed them swiftly. Mom came down from the upstairs with three towels. We quickly wrapped ourselves and sat down at the kitchen table.

"So, Isabella, we never got the chance to ask you, where do you want to live?" I questioned, pulling my green towel closer to my body. She stared at the painted white table for a moment, deep in thought.

"I'm thinking about Kentucky, I think I want to live in Kentucky when I graduate college," she replied sheepishly. A look of confusion swept over Adelaide's face, which was regaining color now that we were warming up.

She asked exactly what I was thinking. "Why the heck would you want to live in Kentucky? Aren't there just a bunch of hillbillies, farmers, and miners out there?"

"Actually, you would be surprised at the number of businesses that are very successful there. It's a beautiful part of the country and, most of all, the future can be bright there if they will do the right things for business. They don't have too many restrictions on business there, and I will own a business someday," Isabella replied in her cute know-it-all voice. Whenever she tells us a fact, she sits a little straighter and gives us this sly smile before she begins talking in a higher pitch voice that is hardly hers.

"Kentucky? Well that's a new one. I have hardly ever heard of a California baby moving to a country state," my mom yelled from the living room, obviously eavesdropping on our conversation.

"Actually, Mrs. DiAngelo, I want to go a place where maybe I can make a difference," Isabella shot back in that voice again. My mom couldn't think of a comeback for that one, so she sat in silence as we made small talk for the rest of the night. Adelaide and Isabella left my house at about midnight to go and see their families.

As I lay in bed that night, trying to fall asleep, my mind began to travel to what life in Kentucky might be like – horses, lakes, streams, hills and river valleys. It was on that day when I remember first considering the Bluegrass state as a potential home.

Isabella began to change my way of thinking that day. I had no idea, at the time, that in a few short years she would change an entire nation's way of thinking.

Capitalism Pointer – Government Rules and Restrictions

Isabella mentioned business rules and restrictions as something she thought about in deciding where to start a business. We need business rules, just like we need rules in other parts of our lives, otherwise we'd have chaos. Is it okay for Isabella to consider whether government rules go too far?

Too many rules, overly complicated rules, and rules which hold businesses back can hurt capitalism and job creation. We have hundreds of thousands of pages of government rules, and we pass thousands of new ones each year. Federal, state and local governments issue new ones all the time, and they rarely go back and take any of the old ones away, so they build up. No one person can know all the rules. Yet businesses which don't follow them can get fined, punished or even shut down.

Think of government rules like speed limits. If you go 90 miles per hour on the highway, most people would agree that's too fast. A speed limit lower than 90 miles an hour is a good thing. But you'd have a hard time getting anywhere if the government issued a new 15 mile per hour speed limit on highways, with the speed limit changing every mile, and with new speed limits coming out every week. You would be confused and it would be difficult to get anywhere on time. You might as well just decide to stay home. Too many rules make businesses stay home by not expanding and hiring more people.

Why do we have so many rules? Human nature makes us want to improve things. Some people think of each new rule as an improvement. They want more and more and more new rules. Everybody who says we need a new rule thinks their new idea will help. Many people who want more rules don't want to hurt businesses and jobs. They just don't understand how capitalism and businesses work. They don't understand that having too many rules can go too far and slow businesses down too much.

What if we added more rules to the games of basketball or soccer each year? What if we first prohibited running but permitted jogging? What if we then prohibited jogging but permitted walking? What if we then decided that the stronger team must give points every game to the weaker team? Pretty soon it would hardly be a game and we wouldn't want to play at all. That's what too many unreasonable government rules can be like for businesses.

With government rules, people think they're making a difference or making progress on one thing, but sometimes they're making bigger problems for other things. Many of the rules have nice sounding names, but has anyone really thought through how they will affect business growth and jobs? Sometimes, no, they haven't.

It's easy to like new government rules because they almost always sound good. For example, in our region of the country we have new drinking water rules that may or may not help. Everybody wants the best water, but the rules will cost every family over $10,000. Federal pension rules require some companies in large pension plans to pay the pensions for employees of other businesses which have gone out of business. Everybody wants everybody to get their pensions, but is it fair to force an employer who has played by the rules to nearly go out of business? It's important to think about the positives and the negatives of government rules.

Federal government rules have made companies which paid to dispose of their waste, at lawful disposal sites, come back later and pay for the clean-up of the sites even though they did nothing wrong. Everybody wants a clean planet, but some of these companies are still paying for waste they disposed of 50 years ago. It would be like the government sending you a $10,000 bill for a car you bought and paid for 10 years ago! Their foreign competitors don't have to pay these amounts because their laws don't put the entire burden on employers. Do you think that's fair?

Sometimes government rules do things to businesses which we would never do to our neighbors. We could write an entire book about government rules. Just know that every new rule usually does a good thing for some people but at the same time it takes away a right or restricts somebody. We should use "critical thinking" with each new rule somebody says we should have. Yes, we need some rules, but do we really need 50,000 pages of federal tax regulations? Probably not.

They Said It Long Ago...

The Role of Government - "A wise and frugal government prevents people from injuring one another, but it otherwise leaves them free to pursue jobs and business...This is good government and it is necessary for our happiness."

—President and Founding Father Thomas Jefferson
(paraphrased)

Freedom - "There can be no liberty unless there is economic liberty."

—British Prime Minister Margaret Thatcher

It's About Families - "When we deprive people of what they have earned, or take away their jobs, we destroy their dignity and undermine their families."

—President Ronald Reagan

And A Famous Joke - "Government's view of the economy could be summed up in a few short phrases: If it moves, tax it. If it keeps moving, regulate it..."

—President Ronald Reagan

Part Three
Make Your Way
In The World!

17

Adelaide Becomes A Student of Life And Work

It's a new decade, the 1990's. It has been four long, hard, school-filled, years and I was finally free! Jake and I graduated from the University of California exactly three days ago and maybe it's just me, but I couldn't wait to get out! Jake, on the other hand, has chosen another year of school to get a Master's Degree in Business. He's going places!

What would my next move be? New York, of course! I figure that after obtaining a college degree in marketing, I just need some experience and some money to get started. For now, I'm saving every dollar I earn working in a Monterey shop, learning everything I can. As soon as I earn the money to pay for an apartment, I will be off to the fashion capital of the U.S.!

Isabella graduated from Yale six days ago. She took Yale by storm. She's now going to work in advanced manufacturing. I think she hopes to rule the manufacturing world someday. She believes she can be a part of turning this country into the world's best place to do business. What a dreamer!

Some people might not like my job. But I love it. I love helping people and, as they say, anything worth doing is worth doing right! It's so exciting to help people find outfits for special occasions or even just helping with seasonal shopping! I'm also training as a manager and helping with the marketing of the shop. Everybody's got to start somewhere. I don't make much money, but I'm learning a lot of things on this job.

For now, I am living with my family until I can raise enough money, but if my calculations are correct, I will be able to go to New York in about six months. I have saved up all my extra money from college jobs and high school for this and I can practically see the light at the end of the tunnel!

"Adelaide! Break's over, time to get back to work," my boss, Kelly, ordered. Wow, had it been fifteen minutes already? I got up from the chair in the break room and entered the main room of the shop. The bright light bounced off the vibrant green walls, blinding me for a second. Loud pop music erupted from the ceiling speakers and I danced over behind the checkout counter. The anxious chatter of customers filled the shop as I began to doodle on the yellow notepad in front of me. Just as I was about to finish a new dress design I heard a familiar voice.

"Hello, do you know of a girl who works here by the name of Adelaide?" the voice asked, obviously trying to use a French accent, but failing.

I pointed to my nametag without looking up, "I am she." For a while, the girl just stood there silently. I finally glanced up to see familiar brown locks with sunglasses hiding the brown eyes that I knew were beneath them.

"Isabella!" I exclaimed, climbing out from behind the counter and wrapping my arms around her tall figure. We hadn't seen one another in years. "What are you doing here?"

"I decided I would pay you a surprise visit…. I also have a gift for you," she whispered in my ear. Now she really had my attention.

Surprise? What surprise? "Really? Why did you bring me a present?" I asked, walking back behind the counter.

"I'll tell you after your shift is over. Meet me at Frozen Berry when you get off work and I will give it to you," she replied, turning and walking out of the shop without another word. I tried to catch her, but she was too quick and I was left there, confused and curious.

18

Isabella Helps A Friend Get Her Start

Ring ring ring, the sharp trill of the bell on the restaurant door filled my ears. I whipped my head around to just the person I wanted to see. Jitters swirled around in my stomach, mixed with nerves of excitement. The blonde came to sit across from me in the bright pink booth. I shoved my hand in my back pocket, in search of the thin paper plane ticket. When my fingertips met with the smooth surface, a smile formed on my thin lips.

"Isabella, stop toying with me. Why are you really here?" Adelaide asked me, a look of question filling her icy blue eyes.

"I already told you. I have a present for my best girl. I think you will really like it," I replied, pulling out the single ticket. Adelaide stared at it for a second in confusion and then sucked in a big gulp of air.

"A plane ticket to New York? Isabella! Why did you do this?" she asked, taking the ticket from me with shaking hands. She examined it gingerly, as if it would suddenly burst into flames if she held it for too long.

I smiled at the longing in her eyes. "I worked at a manufacturing plant while I was going to school – so I could learn about business. I earned money and saved as much of it as I could. My dream is to go to Kentucky. Your dream is to go to New York. This ticket is just a little something for my favorite sister."

"Bella, thank you so much! I will find a way to repay you, I promise," she shouted, making heads turn.

"Shh, calm down. You don't have to repay me. It's a gift and the plane leaves tomorrow, so I suggest you get packing," I told her, smiling. As excited as I was for her, I knew I would miss her. I knew that it would feel as if a piece of me had been taken with her to New York, but this was her dream. Adelaide ran around the table and squeezed me tightly. "Can I help you pack?" I asked.

"Of course you can!" she told me, grabbing my hand and rushing me out of our favorite old hang out.

"Wait, aren't we going to get ice cream?" I asked, but she was intently focused on getting to the car at top speed. Her head did not turn and if she had heard me, she didn't acknowledge it. Without answering me, she piled into the driver's seat of the car and we drove quickly, straight towards the small house.

It wasn't long before I found myself in her room, sitting on the bed staring wide-eyed as Adelaide approved or rejected her clothing. The approved clothes went into the "take to NY" pile and the frowned upon clothes went into the "keep at home" stack. According to Adelaide, the "take" clothes must be professional, not cutesy (which was most of her wardrobe.) All of the professional clothes were folded neatly into Adelaide's three biggest suitcases and placed by the bedroom door.

"Well, I better be going home," I told her when everything was ready. "The plane leaves at noon, so Jake and I will meet you at the airport at 10:30 tomorrow to say goodbye and help you with your bags." She gave me one last hug.

"Thank you, Isabella, for everything!"

And with that, I gave her a tight squeeze and left, excited for my best friend but also dreading tomorrow, the day my best friend would leave to make her way in the biggest city of all.

Capitalism Pointer – Our Opportunities Come From Capitalism

Adelaide got some experience at a California shop and now she's off to New York to pursue her dream job. Isabella helped with money she earned while in college. How do people earn money and where does it come from? The main way people earn money, of course, is from their jobs working for businesses.

The money people earn comes from capitalism. This is easy. A large majority of America's employees work for businesses. Without businesses, people would not have money to build their best tomorrow financially for their families – and there certainly wouldn't be fashion opportunities for Adelaide in New York.

But what about people who work for the government? They do important jobs, but where does their money come from? It comes from tax dollars. Where do tax dollars come from? Businesses pay taxes to pay for government, which means these tax dollars come from capitalism. Employees of businesses pay taxes, which also come from capitalism. People pay taxes based on the property they own or the things they buy, which come from capitalism. You get the idea. Without capitalism, there is no money for government or government employees. This is fact, not fiction.

The next time you hear somebody criticize someone who owns a business, maybe saying they make too much money, just remember....we need them and they need us. Adelaide will never develop her talents without a business which is willing to give her a shot. For anybody who loves government and government employees, they should also really love businesses and business owners. After all, the money for government comes from capitalism and businesses!

If our money and the government's money come from capitalism, wouldn't you expect everybody to like capitalism and to want it to do well? Unfortunately, not everybody sees it that way. A big key to seeing the world in which we live and work is to understand these simple things. You're already well on your way to getting there!

19

Jake Figures It Out

I picked up a dirty pair of pants off my apartment floor and tossed them into the laundry basket. I finally earned enough money to rent my very own apartment, but without anyone to talk to, it's pretty lonely. I absentmindedly twiddled a bolt from the kitchen table between my pointer finger and thumb, listening to the heavy silence. Adelaide went off to New York over a year ago to conquer the fashion world. Isabella flew to Kentucky about three months ago to pursue her dream of opening a company. I'm not exactly sure how she is doing, but I do know that I am alone now.

My two best friends are now halfway across the country, fulfilling their dreams, living their lives, maybe even falling in love. And here I sit, in my small apartment, in my hometown of Monterey. I know I want to get out of this town, but something's holding me back.

I glanced at the bolt in my hand, cringing at the cold metal. Carefully, I bent down and placed it back in its spot right under the front left leg of the table. It snapped in with a satisfying chink, like the last piece to a puzzle. That bolt helped hold the entire table together, and a thought popped into my mind. The bolt fit like the last puzzle piece, the one that has been missing for a long time, but is necessary to complete the picture. A goal.

A dream. A vision. That's my missing puzzle piece. My friends had the drive to get out of California because they had a goal to meet.

That is what I need. But what is my dream? What do I want to do? Who do I really want to be? I crossed out of the kitchen to the bedroom, perplexed, and grabbed my iPod from the bedside table. The comforter sunk as I flopped down onto the bed, pressing the power button on the device. The screen stayed black, not lighting up with light as I had expected. Frustrated, I sigh and press it again. Still nothing.

"Gosh, not this again!" I uttered, out loud. This was not the first time my malfunctioning iPod had refused to come to life and each time, I quietly took the back off and managed to fiddle with it until the screen flashed and came to life. That's when it hit me. I loved fixing things – connecting one thing to another in a new way – thinking of the future. What if I could do something in business with my natural talents?

What if I could get out of this town and invent new software for electronics? The shiny iPod fell onto the comforter with a thud, but I hardly noticed it. I found my dream. I found my drive. I found my goal in life. Now, all I had to do was live it. And that's exactly what I started to do.

20

Adelaide Finds Inspiration

I watched fireworks flash across the sky, raining sparks of red white and blue. I placed my hands against the glass, smiling up at the night sky. People far below cheered with Fourth of July joy as one color after another lit up the darkness. I could faintly hear the boom from inside. I longed to go and celebrate with the carefree New Yorkers.

But I have responsibilities. I now work at one of the highest fashion companies in New York, called Maui Lynn. I am an apprentice designer here and I hope I will soon become a full time designer. Someday I just know I'll manage and run a fashion business.

But for now, I will take anything I can get. Money is tight at this point, but that's nothing new to me. Money has always been a difficult subject for anyone in my family (we never had much) and now is no exception. I gazed at the colors, red, blue, pink, green, white, silver, orange; all symbolizing the hills and valleys in the road of life.

My life is white. I am at a standstill right now, as I wait for the opportunity to make my move and rise up the fashion pyramid. I will wait for my time to come, when the colors will be vibrant magentas and eye catching fuchsias. But for now, white. Blank. It feels like a standstill.

"Adelaide! Where is that belt design? If it's finished by midnight, you can go and watch the end of the fireworks!" Alex, my mentor, yelled from the other room. I sighed and tore myself from the window, shielding my eyes from the blinding lights. I sat down in front of my desk and grabbed the mechanical pencil from behind my ear. A blank sheet of printer paper lay on the mahogany table, constantly reminding me I had a total of … wait for it… zero ideas for this belt. I ran my hand through my blonde curls, closing my eyes in a desperate attempt to find inspiration.

The fireworks flashed under my closed lids and an idea came into my mind. Diamond studded, braided basis, and black belt material. I quickly scribbled a sketch on the white sheet and colored it hastily. When I knew it was finished, I smiled at it, knowing that with a few tweaks and a more detailed drawing, my belt could sell in all the big New York clothing companies.

"Alex! It's done! See ya tomorrow morning!" I yelled, grabbing my faux Gucci bag and slinging it over my shoulder. I impatiently pushed the elevator button, rapidly punching it over and over again. I rode it down the fifty-six floors, listening to the boom of the fireworks outside. The New York air hit me as I exited the skyscraper. The finale of the show was just beginning and the cheers of the observers were almost overwhelming. I couldn't imagine being anywhere else on this beautiful Fourth of July night.

21

Isabella Finds
Her New Home

The muggy August Kentucky air hit me as soon as I got off the plane. I felt the thick humidity fill my nose and mouth. I dragged my bulky bag behind me as I trudged through the airport. I couldn't help but notice a few heads turn as this out of place California girl walked alone through the airport like a lost puppy.

My accent seemed out of place and awkward in the midst of the Southern tones. As I gathered my luggage off the rotating bag carrier, I kept my head down and stared at my shoes. I felt like the escaped orphan from Annie as I loaded myself into a cab.

"Where to, Mam?" the driver questioned.

"Umm..." I paused, trying to remember the address of the condominium I rented not too long ago. "4488 Faring Lane, Florence, Kentucky."

I handed the man my credit card and let him swipe it, crossing my arms across my chest. We sat in silence, letting the radio noise fill the void, for the duration of the ride. After we arrived at the complex, I quickly thanked the man and grabbed my bags from the trunk.

My mind wandered to my Kentucky plans. I carried my bags into the lobby of the condominium complex. Light shone off the striped wallpaper and reflected off the mirror behind the concierge desk. A cute guy with spiked blonde hair and striking blue eyes greeted me.

"Hello, welcome to Bluegrass Condominiums. Are you Isabella?" he asked, flashing a breathtaking smile.

"Ye…Yes" I stammered, placing my bags on the hardwood floor as an excuse to take my eyes off of him.

"Nice to meet you, Miss Waters. I'm Tanner, the caretaker of this beautiful complex. Your room number is…." He paused, rummaging through a pile of papers before pulling out a small plastic card. "363, correct? May I help you with your bags and show you to your room?"

I froze, shocked by his generosity. Not many men today are kind enough to help a woman with her heavy bags – this must be Southern hospitality. "Uh, thank you, Tanner. I would appreciate that." He walked out from behind the desk, the sound of his dress shoes tapping against the wood. As we made our way to the elevator, Tanner asked me what brought me to Kentucky.

"Well, I have been thinking about opening my own business for a while now and I have heard from several people that Kentucky has some of the best opportunities. I applied for and *oops!* received a manufacturing position at Toyota, but I hope this is just the beginning for me. I originally lived in California, where taxes were higher. Taxes in Kentucky, however, are better for businesses, and who knows, maybe someday we can make them even lower so that more and more businesses will come here," I replied, probably giving him more information than he really needed or wanted. He pressed the elevator button and I watched it light up like a Christmas tree.

Tanner paused for a long time, seeming to take in my words. "Well, if those were your reasons for moving, then you will not be disappointed. I assure you, Ms. Waters. Toyota is a great company and we're glad to have you here. We love businesses, and with that kind of attitude, maybe someday you should go into politics."

Politics? I hadn't even succeeded in business yet. We reached the third floor. The long, thin hallway seemed to stretch forever and the flower print wallpaper vined its way onto the high ceilings.

"It's a bit outdated, but you will adjust, everyone does," Tanner murmured as we approached my room. He's right. The hallway is pretty old-fashioned and I'm sure the rooms are not much different, but something about it appealed to me. It reminded me of home. My mom always left our house dated and never renovated anything. After Dad passed away we didn't have much money to update or renovate.

I smiled to myself as Tanner placed the bags in front of room 363. He opened the door with the key and flung the door open, revealing a quaint three-room condo.

"Thank you so much," I told Tanner, smiling graciously as he placed my bags within the doorway.

"Anytime, Ms. Waters. If there is anything you would ever need, you know who to call," giving me two thumbs up. More Southern hospitality.

"Actually," I began. "There is something you could do. Can you tell me the name of the best bank in the area? Someday I'll need a loan to start my own company…."

22

Jake's Big Idea

I fiddled with the wire in my hand, picking at the crimson rubber coating. Shreds of the red material came off in my fingers as I connected the wire to the white one. A sizzle came from the dead computer and the screen flashed blue. But as quickly as it had come, it was gone.

"Not again!" I spat, unplugging the wires hastily. The computer and I have been playing this game for about two hours now. I would plug one wire into another, the screen would flash blue or green, and then it would go black as night.

"Jake, honey, did you get the computer working?" My mom called from the kitchen. An enchanting smell came my way from the kitchen and I resisted the urge to follow the smell. I knew my mother had prepared a special meal for me because I was fixing her computer, but I would not eat until the screen lit up and stayed bright. My stomach growled in protest as I turned back to the darkness.

"Not yet, Mom. It will be soon though, I promise!" I yelled back, picking up the white wire. I thought back to everything I had learned in a college course. *When fixing a computer, the white wire in the monitor always connects with the green... or was it the blue? Or maybe the yellow?* I sighed. I racked my brain for some signal as to which wire would earn me my dinner, but I couldn't think straight.

I guess I will just try them all, I thought, gazing at the white wire. I connected it with the green, but this time, the screen didn't even flash. Next, I tried it with the blue. I was rewarded with a bright blue flash, but as always, the game continued and darkness engulfed the screen once more. I tried the yellow wire. Nothing. *Wait a second,* I thought. *Where is the orange wire?* I dug through the monitor, careful not to disturb any other setups.

A bright orange glare flashed in my peripheral vision and I reached for it. "Yes," I murmured triumphantly as I freed the orange wire from the mess of strings. I took a deep breath and connected the white and orange wire. The screen roared to life, displaying the summer background my mom had plastered onto the screen.

"Did you get it, J?" my mom called again. I got up off my knees and screwed the monitor top back on. I ran towards aroma that came from the kitchen.

"Yes, I did, but that computer is a stubborn little thing, isn't it?" I asked her, grabbing one of her famous oatmeal cookies and taking a small bite, savoring the flavor. "Hey, Mom, I was thinking…," I began.

She poured me a glass of milk. I watched as the creamy liquid filled the clear mug. Mom sat down next to me. "Yes, Honey?"

"I was thinking, while I was fixing the computer, there might be a better way to cause a computer to run, a way without color-coded wires and connecting hard-drives." I told her, flipping my black hair out of my eyes.

My mother pursed her lips, which was her way of saying 'be quiet, I am thinking.' "Do you think," she began. "Do you think you could develop something, a software or design that could eliminate these problems?"

"Yes, Mom, I do. With some work, I think software and new components could link together – no wires, no more headaches." I pushed the last bite of cookie in my mouth, chewing slowly. "Could I," I stuttered, "maybe use your computer as a test drive?"

She gathered my empty plate in her arms, setting it carefully in the sink. "Of course you can! In fact, you can use our basement as your lab and work area. Any day I get to see my boy is a good day."

"Thanks, Mom. Well, I'd better get started. Call me when dinner is ready!"

23

Adelaide Tastes Success

"Adelaide, your belt is a total hit! It's being sold at all the big companies in NYC! I knew you had it in you, Kid!" Alex patted me on the back, flashing me a big grin with her sparkling white teeth. "And as a reward for your hard work, you are now an official designer and manager of a work team here at Maui Lynn!"

I stared at her, wide eyed, as my brain tried to process this new flow of information. "So, so I will get my own office and an apprentice of my own?"

"For the apprentice, you might one day, if you keep working hard and succeeding in your work. As for the office, yes." Alex handed me a set of keys with a keychain that read "Maui Lynn Designer." I took the metal key in my hand and smiled down at the bronze symbol of success.

"Thank you so much!" I yelled, throwing my arms around her. "You won't regret it," I whispered, giving her one last squeeze. I waved her a quick goodbye as I traveled up two floors to my new office. My heart pounded in excitement and my smile only seemed to grow wider. I noticed the key was differently shaped than the one in Alex's office, but I had a little trouble getting the door open. I jiggled the metal key in the key hole until I heard a click.

I flipped my hair out of my eyes and opened the door to the office, revealing the reward for my hard work. Bright sunlight shot through the glass window that covered the left wall, just like the other offices, but that's where the resemblances stopped. The mahogany desk sat right in front of the window, rather than opposite of the glass. Behind the desk sat a black spinning chair, instead of a wooden one. In front were two matching modern chairs for future clients, who I was certain, would come someday.

A tall book case covered a second wall, filled with fashion books and blank sketch pads. The two remaining walls were painted a fashionably noted emerald. The sun reflected off the walls, casting diamonds of light around the room. A single lamp sat on the wood finish of the desk, lighting up at my command. As I approached the desk, I saw a folded sheet of paper lying on the blank surface. My heels clicked softly as I reached for the letter.

Ms. Adelaide Ballou,

You do not know me, but I certainly know you. You are the talk of New York due to your fantastic improvements on the Maui Lynn line. My name is Jacob Garret, creator and designer of Point Blank clothing line. As it appears, you have extreme talents, Ms. Ballou, I was wondering if you would like to attend the Point Blank fashion show with me on the fifteenth of September. I would especially love it if you could design one special outfit to be worn by one of our top models on the runway. I was thinking something flashy and 'in'? The show is at 7pm. I hope to see you there!

RSVP: 546-9785
Jacob Garret
Creator and Designer

This was my chance! This was my chance to finally make it big! If Mr. Garret liked my design, I would be one step closer to opening my own store and my own fashion line. I pulled out my cell phone from my back pocket and dialed the number scrawled on the paper.

"Jacob Garret, creator and designer of Point Blank fashion line, who is this?" he answered in a husky voice.

"Oh, hello, Mr. Garret. This is Adelaide Ballou, designer at Maui Lynn Fashion Company," I replied, twisting a blonde curl in apprehension.

"Oh, Ms. Ballou, it's very nice to finally talk to you. Have you considered my offer?"

"Yes, I have," I paused, "and I would be honored to show a piece of our work at your show."

"Thank you, Ms. Ballou. I am looking forward to meeting you in person. The event is black tie, so make sure to dress nice. See you there." And with that, he hung up.

The line went dead and I closed my flip phone, pushing it back in my pocket. My stomach growled in protest and I glanced at the digital clock sitting on the desk. *12:32. Well, I guess it is lunchtime,* I thought, beginning to make my way out of the office.

I had exactly thirteen days to design and create my outfit. I hesitated at the door, my hand resting on the doorknob. *I should get started*, I told myself. My stomach growled once more. *Eh, it can wait until after lunch, but there will be long nights ahead!*

24

Isabella Takes Another Step Forward

I watched from the waiting room as men hung beautiful stained glass windows on the newly built structure in the lot to the right of the bank. Colors of green, red, and blue caught my eye, reflecting the sunlight like a mirror. An obsidian frame vined its way around the perimeter of the oval window. Three men hammered the glass in place and then stood back to admire their handwork. *It's beautiful*, I thought. *I wonder how they make it...*

"Isabella Waters? The banker can see you now," a polite woman with black hair tied in a tight bun on the top of her head announced. I grabbed my purse from below my chair and took one last glance at the hung windows. *Mesmerizing*, I thought again as I followed the petite woman down a short hallway. "Third door on the left, madam."

The third room was bright, with large windows in the back. The sun dotted the carpeted floor and silhouetted a broad shouldered man sitting in a chair behind the desk. "Ah, Ms. Waters! How very nice it is to finally meet you!" he exclaimed, his voice tinted with British. I shook his outstretched hand, the calluses on his hands suggesting years of labor. I had a feeling he had not been a banker his whole life.

"You, too, Mr. Jenkins," I replied, setting my faux Kate Spade purse next to the chair in front of the desk.

He sat down as well. "So you wish to take out a loan?" he questioned, grabbing out a pad of paper and a red pen.

I shifted uncomfortably in my seat. Going to a bank was new territory for me, especially borrowing money from one. "Yes, sir."

"And how much," he paused, "do you wish to borrow?"

I twiddled with a charm on my silver bracelet draped over my wrist. "Well, I was looking at a small building to rent and open a business of my own. I'll need money to get started, for equipment, furnishing, supplies, and to hire people. So I was thinking maybe $500,000?"

Mr. Jenkins scribbled the number on his notepad, nodding his bald head. "And I assume you know about our interest rates and how much a loan like this will cost?"

"Yes sir, I know inflation and interest rates are low now, so it's a good time to take out a loan......." I dropped my bracelet and twirled a piece of my hair.

"Great, we know you are a bright young woman with a bright future. But we need some things from you before giving you a loan. First, we need to see how you plan to pay this money back, with interest. We'll need to see your business plan and learn about the business you want to go into. Most importantly, you will need to have a down payment on the loan – say 20%. This means you'll need to make sure you've saved quite a bit of money before coming back to us. And of course, unfortunately, that money could be lost if the loan is not re-paid."

He opened the top drawer of his desk and gathered two yellow sheets in his hands. The sheets had all sorts of loan rules on them. He handed me a pen that read "Central Bank." And then he encouraged me by saying, "I know we can do business together, and we want to do business with people like you, Ms. Waters."

"Try again, Ms. Walters. This happens all the time. Don't get discouraged. We appreciate you and your business."

"Thank you, Mr. Jenkins. I will be back. Have a nice day," I told him, picking up my purse and slinging it over my shoulder.

Instead of being discouraged, I pumped my fist in the air and cheered, proud of myself. I was one step closer to doing something with my life in business. I would save money and get a business plan. If I was going to own a business someday I may as well learn now – never give up!

Capitalism Pointer – Low Interest Rates and Low Inflation Can Help Capitalism, Businesses, and Jobs

Isabella went to the bank and commented on "interest rates." Why? Interest is the cost of borrowing money. With a loan, you have to pay the money you borrow back, plus an amount called "interest." High interest rates make it more difficult to pay a loan back. Low interest rates make it easier, and with low interest more business people can take out loans to grow their businesses.

What if you had a great business idea which you thought could make lots of money and provide lots of jobs, but you didn't have the money to make the idea become reality? You might need to have office space for your business, production machines, and employees. Like Isabella, you will need money for those things!

If you wanted to go into business but you didn't have the money, you'd need to go to a bank to get a loan or you'd need to find investors. Your ability to get the loan at a low cost could make or break the business. It could also mean a lot to the people who need the jobs your great business idea will create. With high interest rates, a business could choose not to expand or grow jobs.

Isabella also mentioned inflation. What if you have a great business and to run your great business you need to buy materials from around the country? Let's say the materials cost a dollar today and you've set the prices for your product knowing that your materials will cost a dollar. What if in six months the materials cost two dollars? Suddenly you have to raise your prices to stay in business. Will people buy your products at a higher price? Maybe not.

The higher cost of things in our country is called inflation. With high inflation, people can't buy as much with their money, and it can make doing business more difficult. If you're in business, you'll need customers with money who can buy things!

They Said It Long Ago...

Inflation Robs Us All - "By a continuing process of inflation, governments can confiscate, secretly and unobserved, an important part of the wealth of their citizens."
—John Maynard Keynes

The Expert On How To Cause Harm - "The way to crush people with money is for the government to grind them into nothing through taxation and inflation."
—Vladimir Lenin, Communist Leader
(paraphrased)

And A Joke About Inflation - "Inflation is when you pay fifteen dollars for the ten dollar haircut you used to get for five dollars when you had hair."
—Sam Ewing

25

Jake Takes One Step Forward And One Step Back

I worked all day for a computer company and I worked all night on my inventions. I was getting closer. I cut the blue wire at the base, completely ridding the computer of the cobalt line's functions. I squeezed my eyes shut as I pressed the power button, pleading that it still turned on. The screen lit up with life and I mentally patted myself on the back.

This was the third unnecessary wire that I have cut and if I could just get rid of one more, I think I could replicate and connect everything through software and infrared technology, without any wires. It seemed like all my money was going to more and more computers to experiment on and make this happen. Would it all be worth it?

If I succeed, I can begin to develop entirely new software and connectivity for computer users. I thought for a second, pulling on the white carpet strings, before I picked up the wire cutters and snapped the pink wire. I clicked the power button once more and stared at the black screen.

"No! No, no, no, no!" I yelled, trying to connect the pink wire once more. I tied the pink and yellow wires in a tight knot in a desperate attempt to fix the computer.

"Jake, sweetie, are you okay in there?" my mom called, poking her head past the wall to reveal the face I know so well.

I let my face fall into my hands. "I just broke another computer," I murmured, my words muffled by my hands.

"What was that, Jake?"

I pulled my face from my hands. I watched as her face fell, the mask of happiness disappearing for a split second. As quick as it was gone, it was back.

"Oh, Jake, it's," I cut her off.

"Don't say its fine, Mom. Do you know how much this will cost? It's unfixable. I'm a failure," I ranted, running my hand through my hair.

"Jake, we believe in you. Keep at it. Maybe tomorrow you can go and pick up used computers to experiment on for a cheap price," she suggested with a slight smile. I shrugged and checked the clock mounted on the wall.

"I'm going to get some sleep. I'll see you tomorrow. Night" I brushed by her, my head hanging low.

"Goodnight, sleep tight, Jakey," she whispered, using my old nickname she used to call me when I was feeling down. I gave her a small smile and trudged up the stairs, drained. When I reached my old room, I crashed on the bed, not bothering to change into comfier clothes.

I crawled under the covers and pulled them up to my chin. The walls of the room seemed to begin to close in on me, making me feel trapped. My thoughts were jumbled as I tossed and turned under the blankets.

I desperately racked my brain for something that could help me, but I soon realized this was not like my insignificant issues as a child. This was my life and my future in business – maybe my family's future. I smashed my face in the pillow, biting my lip to muffle the scream that waited to thrash from my mouth. I moaned and turned to face the ceiling once more.

Life won't be easy Jake. Not everything will go the way you will want it to. But the only way you can fulfill your dreams is if you **make** *things go your way.* My father's words came rushing back to me. He always told me I am the only one who can control my life and if I wanted something, I needed to work hard and make it happen. *You've got one life, Jake, and this is it. Make it count.* He would always tell me. And that is exactly what I plan on doing.

26

Adelaide Hits The Big Time?

"Ouch!" I cried. Red blood seeped from the wound that the sharp sewing pin had just created in my skin. I quickly wiped the crimson liquid on a white paper towel that sat near the sewing basket, ignoring the searing pain in my pointer finger. I quickly altered my creation as the model stood like a statue on the pedestal.

"Twenty minutes until show time, ladies!" Mr. Garret called, popping his head into the green room. "How are you doing, Ms. Ballou?" he questioned me.

"I am almost ready. Thank you, Mr. Garret."

"The garment looks divine! I can't wait to see it on the runway!" he complimented, turning away before I could respond to talk to another designer and model pair. I added one last stitch to the red dress and took a step back.

"Give me a spin, Alison," I told the blue-eyed, blond-haired model. She turned slowly on the alteration platform, taking a quick glance in the three sided mirror. I smoothed out a tiny crease on the dress and straightened the diamond studded necklace. "Perfect! Are you ready?"

"Yes, I am. This dress is beautiful, Ms. Ballou," she told me, flashing a garment selling smile. I smiled in appreciation, nodding my head. She stepped off the base, her black heels clicking on the tiled floor. The room shimmered with sparkles that have fallen off the clothes and the smell of perfume wafted from each station.

It was ten minutes until show time and I was ready. I exited the prep room and entered the viewing area. I took my reserved seat, right next to Mr. Garret's, who was sitting directly to the right of the catwalk. My heart rate began to go crazy as the time slipped by…5 minutes, 4 minutes, 3 minutes, 2 minutes, 1 minute….. I bit my lip as Mr. Garret took the stage.

"I'm very glad you all have come to see Point Blank's nightlife collection! Our guest designer for this show is Ms. Adelaide Ballou from Maui Lynn's clothing company." A round of applause made the blood flush to my cheeks. I beamed at the clapping audience as Mr. Garret came near the ending of his opening speech. "Remember, this line is supposed to reflect an amazing night out with the girls, or in the club. So sit back, relax, and enjoy the show!"

Mr. Garret briskly came to take his seat next to me, taking a deep breath when he sat down. Loud music blared through the speakers, the kind you would hear in a high-end club. Colored strobe lights flashed from the lamps that hung from the ceiling, matching the beat of the music.

The first model strutted out onto the runway. The beautiful, tan skinned brunette rocked a red flouncy blouse with a black miniskirt topped with a white studded belt looped around her nonexistent stomach. An uncountable number of models followed the brunette before it finally got to my design.

The last remaining model, a blonde-haired beauty, appeared from backstage right. The red dress fit her curvy stature perfectly. A cherry halter strap was stitched to the corners of the sweetheart neckline, forbidding the dress from sliding down. Halfway down her torso was a shiny silver belt. The dress then continued down to the middle of the thighs, stopping in the front but continuing to the floor in the back. Ruffles dotted at the bottom of the garment brushed the catwalk. Her silver heels reflected off the changing lights, forming sparkles on the runway.

When the model reached the end she struck a pose, resulting in an astounding round of applause from the audience. She exited the stage, her dress flowing behind her and the audience cheered once more. I grinned, so proud of my work. The music stopped, the lights turned a light shade of gold and Mr. Garret stepped up once again.

"Thank you all for coming! I really hope you enjoyed our show!" And it was over. Just like that. All the fame I felt not as much as two minutes ago disappeared. I stood for a second, awkwardly twisting my bracelet, wondering if anyone was going to acknowledge my work. But nobody came.

I walked into the crowd of people, desperately hoping that somebody, anybody, would tell me my design was a hit. But it seemed as if no one made the connection between the design and the designer. The black doors neared me and I reluctantly gave up, believing nobody recognized me. I exited the building into the nightly fall air of New York. I stood outside the door, debating if I should go back inside and try again. A yellow taxi cab pulled up to the curb.

"You need a ride, Miss?" he asked with a heavy Bronx accent.

I made my decision quickly. "Thank you," I whispered, making it barely audible. The black leather seats of the taxi were just like every other public transportation car in this city.

"Where to, Miss?" I quickly told him the address and waited patiently as we drove. A single star was visible in the night sky. I smiled to myself, for a star was a rare sight in New York because of all the bright city lights. That was the one thing I missed about Monterey, the stars.

As the star shone faintly, my heart felt a pang of homesickness. Part of me wanted to go home, but I knew that if I left now, I would have to start at the bottom all over again. The car came to a sudden stop and it took me a second to realize we had arrived at my apartment. I quickly thanked the kind man and paid him. He drove off as I stared at the single star. The light faded in and out, like my fame it seemed.

One minute, I was at the top and the next, it was like nobody knew the lonely French girl with long blonde curls that had never been dyed. The homesickness returned as I entered my apartment. I fell on the bed, my dress flailing out to the sides. I grabbed my clutch I had thrown on the table when I walked in and took out my flip phone. I knew who I wanted to talk to, the perfect person who knew exactly how to cheer me up.

"Jake? Hi, it's Addie."

27

Isabella Prepares To Bet It All On A Business Dream

Perfect. That's what this building was. Absolutely, completely, perfect. It was large and rectangular, with an abstract roof to catch people's attention. There was a blank sign in the large front lawn so everyone would know where my company was located. Small, circular windows were scattered across the sides of the building, letting the sun shine on the empty floors. There was a "for sale" sign stuck in the green grass in the very front of the lot. The realtor said the building could be leased for $5,000 a month. This was my building. This was the perfect place to begin building my glass company.

Several years ago, a little after I had seen the men hanging the stained glass windows, I knew that I wanted to manufacture glass. The ways that you can bend, shape, and stain glass while it's still hot are unbelievable! I kept working in my job at Toyota during the day. I learned about manufacturing and management, then at night I learned all I could about the glass business, saving every penny for a down payment so I could get a loan to start the company.

I pulled out my cell phone and dialed the number of my realtor, who I hired maybe three days ago.

"Ms. Waters! I hoped I would hear from you sometime soon! Have you found the building I suggested for you?" I could hear the realtor's signature smile through the phone.

"Yes, and I would like to say, Mrs. Maines, it is exactly what I'm looking for," I told her.

I heard a rustling of stuff in the background through the phone. She was gathering her papers. "Okay, I will be right over to the property. I really hope we can make this work for you!"

"Me, too," I whispered, but she was already gone. I put my phone away and took another lap around the building as I waited. Eventually, a tiny blue Volkswagen Bug pulled into the drive. Out came Mrs. Maines, with her old fashioned, bright red, beehive hairdo and too much red lipstick. When I first met her, I had my doubts, as any normal person would, but Tanner had assured me she's the best in the business.

"I just knew you would love it!" she called, hobbling over in her heels. The wrinkles on her aged face crinkled up as she beamed at me from across the lawn. "So the asking price is $5,000 a month to rent the building, which is pretty high, so I was thinking we could shoot a little lower?

The next day, the phone rang loudly and I dove for it, picking up hastily.

"Hello?" I answered, trying hard to hide the urgency in my voice.

"Isabella…." It was Mrs. Maines on the other line. Her voice hinted at defeat and fatigue. *Oh, gosh. This doesn't sound good*, I thought, biting the inside of my cheek.

"Did you get the property?" I asked, afraid of the answer. I wanted nothing more than for the answer to be yes.

"Well…. That's the thing," she paused and I felt my heart rate speed up. "There was a guy, a businessman, who came in at the last minute and offered full price for the lot and building. I had it under lock and key just before he showed up. I'm really sorry, Isabella. But there's nothing I can do about it."

I have been looking…," her squeaky voice trailed off and I became lost in my own thoughts. She lost the property? The perfect property for my company? How could she let this happen? I knew that it wasn't necessarily her fault but at the moment, I just wanted someone to blame besides myself. I grabbed a pillow off my bed and chucked it across the room. It hit the counter top and slid to land in the chrome sink. Her voice came back into focus "just a few miles from here. I think that it will be even better than the other property and it's only $4,500 a month."

"Okay, can we go on Wednesday?" I asked, trying to keep the bubbling anger out of my voice.

"Wednesday is perfect! The address is 5378 Oakguard Ct, Hebron, Kentucky. See you there!" And with that, the line went dead. I slammed my phone shut and set it on the wooden table. I threw myself onto my bed and wanted to pound the mattress. Didn't she understand I didn't want another property? I wanted that one! An old saying my mom used to tell me when I was really little popped back into my mind, 'you get what you get and you don't throw a fit.' Words to live by in business – at least sometimes!

28

Jake Did It!

After years of trying to invent something that would change the world of computers, I did it! The funny thing about it is that I was down to my last dollar and just about to give up when it finally worked. While friends were buying fancy cars and going to nice restaurants, I was spending every dollar I had on computers and research to make this invention work. Don't get me wrong – I enjoyed working on it – and I'm not complaining, but I had to give up a lot to get my start in business.

The break through happened after I had hardly slept for a week – up all night to make it work. The new software works perfectly. It will make computers even less expensive and they'll work better.

The one question still remaining is where am I going to start this company? I was talking to Isabella a few days ago and she said she finally scored an amazing property for her company in Kentucky. People helped her there – they wanted her to start her business!

They have organizations like the Northern Kentucky Chamber, the Tri-County Economic Development Corporation, and the Northern Kentucky Area Development District which practically rolled out the red carpet for her. Everybody was working together to help. I wonder if they'll do the same for me.

She also told me tax rates are lower in Kentucky than they are in California, which leads me to think Kentucky would be a good place to start a new business. All new companies struggle at first and need all the help they can get. It would be stupid for me to think mine won't.

I'm looking forward to getting away from home anyway and this is my chance. This is my big break, as Addie would call it. I sat on my bed in my small apartment with a restored, but beat up old laptop sitting in front of me. I opened the laptop and got on internet explorer. I typed 'plane tickets to Kentucky from California' into the search box and waited.

But one big question still rattled my brain, where in Kentucky was I planning to move? Well, Bella moved to Northern Kentucky and she seems to love it there… so maybe I could love it there, too! I changed the search to 'plane tickets to Northern Kentucky from Monterey, California.'

I clicked on a website for airline tickets and purchased a ticket for the flight in three days to an airport called CVG, located in Northern Kentucky. That should give me just enough time to pack up my apartment and say my goodbyes. I can't believe that less than a month ago, I was laying on my old bed at my mother's house, beating myself up over a simple mistake. And now, in three short days, I will be on my way to Kentucky to try to start my own business. I was so close. I could practically taste victory.

29

A New Business Seed Is Planted For Adelaide

"Your dress was just divine, Adelaide! Really, truly amazing." Mr. Garret sat right across from me at Nana's, a well-known restaurant in the outskirts of New York City. We sat at a table in a very secluded area, with rows and rows of stacked white roses blocking the view of other customers.

The sun shone through the open ceiling, making the smooth skin on Mr. Garret's face sparkle. I hadn't heard from him since before the show and I had honestly believed that he hated my dress and never wanted to speak to me again. But I guess I was just being paranoid because here he was, praising me on my astounding dress design!

"Have you ever thought about opening your own line and maybe even a chain of shops?" he asked, in his strong Bronx accent. When I finally decoded the sentence, it took me a minute to figure out the answer. Honestly, in the back of my mind, I had wanted to open my own fashion line and shops for years. But I knew that first I'd need to try to make a living and do something people would notice in the fashion industry. Maybe working nearly 60 hours a week for so many years (although I loved most every minute of it), was finally paying off in an American dream.

"I don't know. Do you think I could pull it off?" I asked, almost scared of his answer.

"Do I think you could pull it off? Of course I do! With your amazing design and business skills, your line could be one of the most successful lines in the country! Maybe even more so than mine!" he praised.

My fork almost fell out of my hand, I was so excited. One of the most renowned fashion designers just said that my designs could be better than his! I took a deep breath and composed myself, willing my voice not to sound too ecstatic.

"And how would I go about starting my own line?"

"Well, first, you would need to develop twenty more designs to start off your line. Then, you need to think of a professional and unforgettable name, something that sticks. Next, you purchase or rent shops and buildings to start off your company. Last, you advertise, sell, and become famous!" He laughed and I laughed with him, our laughter ringing throughout the isolated area.

"Excuse me, Mam?" I hailed the waitress over to our table. "May I have the check?"

"Yes, right away, Madame." The pretty fair haired waitress hurried away.

"Let me pay, Adelaide. It's the least I can do for a future star like you," Mr. Garret pleaded. I began to argue, but the waitress brought the check to the table and he snatched it up before I could get to it. "So about that line?" he asked, handing the check back to the waitress.

"Count me in. I'll do whatever it takes," I replied, twisting my Pandora bracelet, which had been a gift from Alex after I became a designer. The waitress brought Mr. Garret's credit card back to him and I knew that it was time to leave.

"Mr. Garret, you've made a difference in my life. You gave me a chance. You encouraged me and I won't let you down." I told him, grabbing my snake skin purse and slinging it over my shoulder. A patch of my blonde curls got caught and I pulled it out from underneath the strap.

"Yes, very nice. If you ever need anything, feel free to give me a call. And think about that line!" He called out, flashing me one last designer cocky smile and left the restaurant. I followed him out, already planning new designs in my head.

Part Four
It's Time To Lead!

30

Isabella Starts Hiring People, Making A Difference In Their Lives

The nippy November air made me pull my jacket tighter over my lean torso. I taped a sign up to the telephone post on Ninth Street in Cincinnati. The sign read 'HELP WANTED' in bold black print. So far, I received five calls from Northern Kentucky and only one from Cincinnati.

Less than a week ago, I finished furnishing my glass company's building. It's now fully equipped with smelting machines, fire pits, kilns, and other instruments used to create glass windows and objects. We have two completely furnished offices, one for me and one for the manager that I will assign once the business is up and running. It will take me years to pay off my business loan and start making real money, but I know it will be worth it.

As I hung the signs, I realized that by opening this business, someday I would be hoping to create jobs for hundreds, maybe thousands, of people and their families. I remember from college this was part of what we call capitalism. The unemployment rate in our area, right now, is very high, so if my business is successful then it will provide food and clothing to many people!

I plastered one last sign to a half-broken window of a rundown storefront. *Well, that's it. There are now seventy five signs hung up in Cincinnati. I've posted the jobs online and contacted the local Chambers of Commerce. I wonder how many calls I will get....?*

Suddenly, I heard a large crash behind me and I spun around, searching for the source of the noise. I clutched my purse tighter to my chest, wrapping the strap around my torso. My eyes stopped at a fallen over trash can on the sidewalk across the street. A masked animal dug through the fallen trash. I relaxed. *It was just a raccoon. Phew.*

Despite knowing that I was not in danger, I hurried back to my car. I drove past old, dilapidated buildings, my grip on the steering wheel lessening as we exited downtown. Suddenly, my cell phone rang and I dug through my purse to retrieve it.

"Hello?" I answered.

"Is this Isabella Waters?" the person on the other end answered. It was a young woman.

"Yes, it is."

The woman seemed nervous as she answered. "Well, I saw one of your flyers in Cincinnati and I was wondering if I could get maybe an interview or something."

My face brightened into a smile. "Actually, we are having an informational meeting on the fourteenth of December. Come over, fill out a job application, and if it looks good I'll be in touch about the meeting."

"Oh! That sounds great!" she enthused.

"The address is 5378 Oakguard Ct, Hebron," I told her, merging into the next lane.

"Great! My name is Abby! I'll see you there," she said.

"I can't wait to meet you, Abby," I replied. I hung up the phone just as I crossed over the bridge. Just on the car ride home, I got three more calls just like that one. Tonight, I got seven more calls from Northern Kentucky. At this rate, the conference room will be packed for the meeting!

The clock on the stove read 11:07 p.m. *I should probably be getting to bed.* I climbed under the covers, already in my pajamas when I heard the sharp trill of my cell. *Must be another caller,* I thought to myself. When I picked up the phone I heard a familiar voice on the other end.

"Hello?" I answered.

"Bella! Hi, it's Jake. If you're so sure that people can make it in business in Kentucky, then I'm moving to Kentucky!" he told me. I was so shocked, I almost dropped my phone. Literally.

31

Jake and Isabella Make A Kentucky Connection

I picked up a heavy bag from the trunk and dragged it into the lobby with my other three bags. A man with short brown hair sat behind the desk in the entrance hall of the condominium complex.

"You must be Jacob DiAngelo?" the man asked.

"Yes, I am, sir," I replied. Just as I said that, I heard an excited scream come from the steps. I would know that scream from anywhere. There was a familiar whoosh of brown hair and a flash of big brown eyes. *Isabella,* I smiled to myself as I grabbed my room key from the man. It read 243, which meant I was just a floor below Isabella. I felt Isabella's arms wrap themselves around my neck as she enveloped me in a bone crushing hug.

"I haven't seen you in forever!" she enthused, squeezing me even harder.

I wiggled out of the hug and turned around to face her. "I know I rea.." Suddenly, my train of thought disappeared as I met her eyes. *Wow....* was the only word to describe her right now. Her face had lost all of the high school baby fat and had become more angular and defined. Her naturally straight hair was full and shiny, framing her face perfectly.

Her skinny figure from high school and college had developed some curves over the years. The deathly pale skin from all the years had become a glowing golden brown. That unpopular little girl with no friends had become, well, a beautiful woman.

"You look like you need a drink of water, Jake," she told me and I realized I had been staring. She giggled to herself and picked up two of my bags. The man behind the desk and I picked up two as well.

"Thank you," I told him, starting up the stairs right behind Isabella. "So does this complex have an elevator?"

"Yes, but you're just on the second floor, let's take the steps," Isabella enthused, running up the stairs with the bags slung over her shoulder. I was glad to know she hadn't changed too much. When we reached my room, Isabella, the man behind the concierge's desk, whose name I found out was Tanner, and I placed the bags right inside the doorway,

"Thanks for helping us, Tanner," Isabella commented. He tipped his hat to us and began the trek back down the steps. The condominium was already furnished so Isabella and I sat down on the plush couch.

"So, watchaya been up to?" I asked her.

"Well, I'm actually on the verge of opening my own glass-making business. I haven't settled on a catchy name yet for the chain of stores where we'll sell the glass. Do you have any ideas?" she asked me, raising both her eyebrows and giving me a shy smile.

I looked at how beautiful she had become and said "Well….. You could go with 'Glamorous Glass,'" I told her, jokingly.

She slapped me lightly on the arm. "Are you calling me glamorous?" she asked, letting out a loud laugh. "You have no idea Jake – my life isn't glamorous – I worked in manufacturing for years, saving money to open my own business, then I had to study the business at night to even have a shot at it. Now my time has come – at least I hope it has!"

"Maybe I am calling you glamorous, maybe I'm not. But seriously, it's catchy! You could have a cool song and a catch phrase and a slogan," I told her, a little more serious this time.

She got up off the couch, stretching. "I'll consider it. But Jake, you've been here less than an hour and you're already trying to name my company!"

32

Adelaide Opens Her First Store

I watched as the sun glinted off the large pair of silver scissors. The red ribbon on the store front held strong, though the wind beat furiously at the strip of fabric. My curls blew wildly and I knew the draft was ruining my straightened hair, tying it in multiple knots. The entire fashion world seemed to be staring at me, their eyes sensing my nervousness. I was about to cut the ribbon to open my very own store and everybody important was coming to judge my work.

The tall, abstract building stood behind me, right on the corner to the right of Times Square. Mr. Garret, who has now become one of my closest friends, signaled for me to come up and make my speech. I smiled at him and he gave me a small thumbs up.

I adjusted the microphone so that it hovered right in front of my mouth. "These past several years have been crazy. One minute, I'm just a small town girl from California with knock off Jessica Simpson heels and Louis Vuitton handbags. And I just can't believe that I am standing here, with some of the world's most noted fashion designers, talking to all of you. This could only happen in America, but even in America, I know that

I couldn't have done this without the help of my mentor, Mr. Jacob Garret."

"He was the one who gave me the spectacular opportunity to do a fashion show and he encouraged me to start my own company. And that is why today, I would like him to cut the ribbon," a round of applause erupted from the audience. "As you all may know, I am originally from the beautiful, fashion capital of the world known as Paris. To honor my hometown, I have named my line, and this shop 'Summer in Paris.'"

"Even though I spent only a few summers in Paris, the memory of that city's beauty has never left me. It inspires me. I remember, like yesterday, the sun glinting off the Eiffel Tower, with people strolling around the streets like they didn't have a care in the world. I hope to go back there someday soon and spread my company to the world. So, without further adieu, I present to you 'Summer in Paris!'"

My heart pounded one last time as Mr. Garret cut the ribbon, causing an eruption from the audience. I watched as famous designers and photographers filed into my boutique. I spotted Alex in the corner of the room, shifting through a rack full of different colored miniskirts. A tall man, who I did not recognize, was talking to the cashier behind the desk.

I hired the cashier just a few days before the opening. She was tall with a full head of black hair. Her bangs fell right above her green eyes. She had just moved to New York and kind of reminded me of myself when I was her age. It felt good to give the girl a shot. I could tell she needed it to get on her feet. All of the clerks and workers had the same dream she and I shared. They wanted to do what I had done and I intend to help them all get there.

A few people came up to me and congratulated me on my success and asked me what I wanted to do in the future. I would always tell them, "I want to expand my business around the world." And they would smile and wish me luck. I knew a few of them still doubted me, but I believed it would happen.

I walked around the store for the next few hours, asking people if they needed help or answering questions for other curious designers. Before I knew it, it was already closing time. Mr. Garret helped me shoo some people out the door, handing them their last shopping bags. It felt so good to see my company's name written in bright pink and green letters on those plastic bags. When the last customer exited through the doors, I turned around, stunned to see that most of the racks were almost empty.

"Katie, did those shipments come in?" I called out to the red haired clerk.

"Yes! They are right in the back," she told me. Mr. Garret came with me to help unpack the overflowing boxes in the storage room.

"So, today was a success?" he asked, wanting my opinion, but already knowing the answer.

"Much more of a success than I expected. I didn't think so many people would show up..." I trailed off, picking up a box marked 'black heels.' Mr. Garret carried a large box into the shop, leaving me in silence. As I unloaded the heels onto the stand, I began to wonder if my goal of having shops around the world was kind of far-fetched. I pondered over the thought for a bit before running into Mr. Garret again.

"Hey, do you think my dream for expanding my company is outrageous?" I asked him, looking up into his brown eyes.

"Outrageous? As if! You're Adelaide. With you in charge, anything's possible."

33

Glamorous Glass Grows More and More Jobs

Valentine's Day- A day full of romance and people doing sweet things for one another. But I don't have that one special person in my life to give anything to and I don't expect anything. Let's just say I don't anticipate roses or a card. Anyway, I don't have any time for stuff like that today. It's been about three years since I first opened my glass company. Believe it or not, I went with 'Glamorous Glass.' Jake was overjoyed with my decision and even helped me design the sign out front.

As my company grew bigger and bigger and our name got out to the world, I realized I needed more workers. So today, I had interviews with over twenty possible employees, all of whom needed a job. I was tempted to give them each a job, but then I realized I couldn't afford to pay all of those people. I planned to hire ten to fifteen workers. I twiddled a pen in my hand, listening to the hypnotizing sound of it hitting the wooden desk. I pulled down the hem of my black business pencil skirt when I heard a knock on the door, signaling the first person up for the interview.

"Happy Valentine's Day!" a perky brunette said to me. She obviously enjoyed the idea of having an entire day devoted to love and romance. I picked up the resume' of the girl and saw the name was Sarah Jenell. Sarah Jenell? Where have I heard that name before?

"You, too," I replied, still wondering who this girl was and where I knew her from. "It's nice to meet you, Ms. Jenell."

"Oh, you, too, Ms. Waters," she replied.

"Please, have a seat," I told her. She followed my orders and sat down in the single chair in front of the desk. She crossed her legs, making sure I noticed her six inch pumps. "So, tell me about yourself."

"Well, I grew up in Monterey, California and now I live here, as a single mom with my two beautiful children," she kept rambling, but that's when it hit me. This was one of the girls in the clique that used to pick on me for not having the newest clothes or books.

I remember clearly now. Sarah Jenell, the queen bee, partner in crime, co-captain of the cheerleading squad, great with comebacks and insults, but not the smartest kid in our class. And here she was, the girl who had made my elementary school years a living hell, asking ME for a job. I zoned back into her speaking.

"And I'm just trying to give a good life to my children because I know how important school and a good home are for a future."

"And do you have any experience in glasswork?" I asked, trying to block out the parts of her history I had suddenly remembered.

She seemed nervous to answer this question, for she twirled a strand of her hair around her neatly painted fingernail. "Well, I took a few business classes before I applied here, so I know about business. I know it's not much, but I will take more classes and training sessions – whatever it takes," she pleaded. And at that moment, I really believed her.

"Thank you so much, Ms. Jenell. I will get back to you on it by tomorrow night," I replied, scribbling some more stuff on the back of her headshot. She began to gather her things and leave, but she paused at the door.

"I'm sorry, Isabella, for what I did in elementary school. It was stupid and I was just being arrogant," she apologized.

"All is forgiven – let's focus on the here and now and see what we can do to grow this business, with you possibly as a member of the Glamorous Glass team," I replied.

Her face lit up with gratitude. "Thank you so much. I'm really glad we cleared things up."

"Yes, me, too." I agreed. She quickly left, and I pondered whether to give her the job. It wasn't long before I heard yet another knock on the door and I realized I had more interviews.

"Come in!" I said, praying it wouldn't be another blast from the past. I thought to myself, I must always be looking to the future – not back to elementary school.

At the end of that long day, I noticed an unopened envelope on my desk. Not knowing who left it or where it came from, I opened it slowly. Someone had remembered me after all. It was a simple, handwritten Valentine from Jake.

> *A part of me has loved you since the first day I saw you on the beach in Monterey. I've been afraid to admit it until now. Isabella, will you be my Valentine today, tomorrow, and hopefully forever?*

Capitalism Pointer – Everybody Should Root For One Another

Isabella's meeting with Sarah Jennel is a pretty good example of how we should be rooting for one another in this country. Things hadn't turned out well so far for the once popular Sarah. Being the most "popular" person in elementary and high school has very little to do with success in life!

Sarah could have chosen to be jealous of Isabella's success, but instead she came to Isabella for a job. If Isabella had never succeeded, Sarah would have lost out on a job opportunity. In the end, Isabella rooted for Sarah and Sarah rooted for Isabella. They healed an old wound and went forward.

In this country we should be cheering for all people, including people who earn more money than us. These "rich people" help us all, sometimes in ways you wouldn't think about. For example, a family with money could buy a new hot tub, or it could decide not to buy one. Lots of items go into a hot tub. Everybody who makes one of these items has a job because people buy hot tubs.

Tens of thousands of people in this country have jobs because of hot tubs - and the people who buy them. If we have fewer people who can afford a hot tub, people will lose jobs. If you care about the people who have jobs working on things like hot tubs, root for them and root for people who have enough money to buy things!

With capitalism, people don't usually become poor because someone else becomes wealthy. If millions of people come up with new ideas for products and they do a great job with them, millions more people can do well. When more people do well and go into business, they can hire even more people who can do better. There's always room in America for the next great idea which makes lots of people do better.

Think of Microsoft and Apple. They sell the computer systems all over the world and much of that money comes back to our country! Hundreds of thousands of people in our country have good jobs because of them. The next time you hear someone criticize people because they have money, or say that they have too much money, consider telling them we should be rooting for everybody. That's when America's at its best!

They Said It Long Ago...

We're In This Together - "You cannot help the poor by destroying the rich...You cannot lift the wage earner up by pulling the wage payer down...you cannot build character and courage by taking away people's initiative and independence. You cannot help people permanently by doing for them, what they could and should do for themselves."

—President Abraham Lincoln

34

Isabella Runs Into American Business Problems

Alright, let me just start by saying that I knew starting a company would be difficult, but I truly thought that I would have more opportunities than problems, not the other way around!

If you haven't been living under a rock, you know that we're not the only country which manufactures and sells glass. Manufacturers from China have stepped in. And the thing that irritates me the most is that we lost business to the Chinese because their employees work for almost nothing.

But I'm not the kind of person who gives up at the slightest hint of trouble. With a little bit of research, my team and I figured out there are types of glass China can't produce very well. Would it have been nice to have been able to sell all types of glass? Well, of course, but that goal is just a few feet short of impossible. Since I can't win that battle, I've been thinking about opening up new glass shops overseas in places like England, Africa, and China. I'll show them who's boss.

Problem number two- when the Chinese took some of our glass business away, I had to let workers go because we didn't have enough work for them. It hurt me to see those people struggling to make ends meet without the job that I provided for them. Hopefully, sometime in the near future, I can rehire them to help out.

And to top it all off, we just got finished with a major lawsuit. When I fired a Chinese worker who had immigrated to the Americas, he sued me for racial discrimination! That was not what I meant when I fired him! In all truth, I forgot he was Chinese and laid him off because his glass quotas were lower than some of my more experienced workers. On the bright note of my story, we won the lawsuit. Whoop-de-do.

What's my plan? To keep moving forward. Yes, these things will slow our growth and we won't be hiring as many new employees next year. But give up? Yeah, right!

Capitalism Pointer – Worldwide Business And Lawsuits

Isabella talked about competing with companies in other countries, such as China. Many of our businesses are "international" because they sell products in other countries, or they buy supplies from other countries. Businesses here decide to open plants in other countries and businesses in other countries open plants in America. International business both helps and hurts American businesses and jobs. We have more people to sell to around the world, but we also have more competitors around the world!

One of the best things about international business is something people don't usually think about. If companies all over the world have to compete to provide you with the best and least expensive product, chances are, you'll get the best and least expensive product. When you go to a department store, if you look closely you can find products made all over the world. The companies which produced those products probably got their items into the department store because they were the best and least expensive.

Without international business, the things we buy wouldn't be as good or as inexpensive. This gives us better things which cost less, which means we have more money left over to spend on other things or to save. Think of it this way. With international business, we have the whole world trying to do their best to make sure we're satisfied with the things we buy. This has happened in the automobile industry, for example, where great foreign cars came into America and our companies started making American cars better. We had to keep up or go out of the car business!

Because many businesses compete all over the world, we can't keep American jobs unless we compete and win quite a bit of the time against businesses in foreign countries. We must produce better and/or less expensive goods, or we lose jobs. For several reasons, this has been a big challenge for our country. Our country has higher taxes and more rules than many countries. It's not surprising that some businesses have left the United States. We must compete with other nations, who may have fewer rules and lower taxes, to keep our jobs. On the other hand, companies from other countries have decided to open plants here to be closer to their American customers.

The bottom line is that we win some and lose some with international competition. Isabella lost some business to China, and some people lost their jobs, but she's trying to get more business by winning in other countries. In the end, it's up to us to make America the greatest place to do business in the world - so more and more people want to do business here. With this approach, we can make sure we have the very best jobs and opportunities.

As for the lawsuit Isabella faced, businesses have to pay for attorneys and court costs when they're sued. For a small company, this can wipe out much of their profit for a year, even if they did nothing wrong. In this country, no one reimburses a business for its costs in defending a lawsuit brought by one of its former employees. Even if, in Isabella's case, she did nothing wrong, she still has to pay, win or lose. And if she loses, she must pay the former employee's costs and attorneys' fees.

Other countries don't do it this way. But in this country, more or less, people do have the right to sue one another. Defending yourself and getting "justice" can be expensive. In Isabella's example, if she hadn't fired some employees after she lost the China business, who knows, maybe she would have gone out of business. If this happened, then all of her employees would have lost their jobs.

Isabella didn't fire the employees because she wanted to or because she was a bad person. You can't keep paying people when there's no work to do. But she got sued anyway, and paid a hefty price for defending herself. That doesn't seem fair, does it?

They Said It Long Ago...

Businesses Deserve Justice Too - "Capital (business) has its rights, which are as worthy of protection as any other right."
—*President Abraham Lincoln*

35

Jake Sees How His Business Can Help People

I glanced around the empty store. It was 7:30 a.m., exactly thirty minutes before the store would open. We have been in business for two years now. The employees were in the back, waiting for opening time. Yesterday, I talked to them about investing more of the money I'd saved to run more television commercials and to do more advertising. Sometimes you just have to spend money to make it.

Our software sales are going well online and in our store, but I remember our first day in business when we sold only four units, which was not exactly what I expected. Let's just say I wasn't an overnight success. As we tried to grow, we also decided to go into the computer repair business. Yesterday we repaired ten laptops! The work was hard and frustrating, but boy, does it pay well!

I walked out into the mall hallway (my store was in a big section of the Florence Mall) and glanced around. I saw elderly men and woman walking up and down the stairs, trying to get their exercise in before the shops open in the mall today. Everything seemed so quiet. Nobody was in a hurry or looked like they had somewhere else they had to be. It was actually pretty peaceful.

Across the mall was a man setting up an iPhone case stand, getting ready for the day. Below was the empty Florence Mall playground set for the little kids to play on. The mall felt strange, being all empty like this. I sighed and check my watch. *7:56, I'd better get to work*, I thought, walking back into the fluorescently lit store. I pulled up the gate from inside and called out the workers.

They silently took up their positions, a few boys still playing on their phones. I hired people from Northern Kentucky who had experience in computer diagnostics. Every single one of them can repair just about any broken laptop in under two hours, depending on the problem with the computer. 9:00 a.m. rolled around and I saw a customer stroll in.

It was an older lady. Her white hair was thinning and her round glasses sat on top of her pointy nose. Her frail hands held a beat up laptop. The computer looked like someone had a panic attack and launched it halfway across the world.

"What can I help you with, mam?" I asked her.

Her voice reflected her brittle appearance. "Well," she started. "I was wondering if you could fix my computer."

I stared at her, at first, wondering if she was serious about fixing this ancient computer. I replied as calmly as I could. "I'm not sure if this computer is fixable, but I can replace it with a new computer which has better software, so your problem will be fixed."

Her tone was airy and frail. "I like this computer. I've had it for years. Are you sure there's no way you can fix it?" she pleaded.

"I can try," I told the elderly woman. She nodded and thanked me, placing the laptop on a nearby table. She took my hand in both of hers.

"So if you could come back tomorrow, I'll let you know how we did," I replied. She thanked me once again and exited the shop.

I stayed up half the night trying to fix the nice lady's computer before finally getting it to work. Around 4:00 a.m., it slowly (but surely) growled to life.

The next day, it was about halfway through the day and she hadn't come back in yet. I kept a close eye out for a flash of white hair or the sight of skin sticking to thin bones. But she didn't show. Just as I was beginning to worry, someone tapped me on the shoulder.

"How is my computer doing?" she asked, her voice shaking.

"Well, it works once again," I replied. I'm not sure what I was expecting, but she wrapped her thin arms around my stomach and hugged me, laughing an old lady chuckle.

Capitalism Pointer - Capitalism Makes Things We Need and Want

Jake wanted to help his business so he decided to help people fix their computers. With capitalism, hundreds of thousands of people like Jake are trying to figure out what we need and want. New things come out all the time – from the latest video game, the latest movie, or the latest fashion. We have so many choices available to us that it's hard to even keep up with all of them. Choices are a good thing!

How does all this happen? It happens because of capitalism. It's actually amazing when you think about it. Businesses, every minute of every day, all around the world, are trying to provide things you want. This only happens through capitalism.

With capitalism, business people will always be looking for the next great idea or a new way to improve things. Meanwhile, employees who make the products you buy have jobs to help their families. Everybody wins!

Countries which haven't had capitalism have seen that even getting something as simple as toilet paper can become very difficult. Without capitalism, people don't have big incentives to deliver choices to consumers. But with capitalism and freedom, many people will want to start businesses to make profits. They will invent new, amazing things which will come to a store near you - it's guaranteed.

But it's not just about the choices we have. It's about the quality of the things we can buy. With capitalism, businesses will usually want you to like their products and buy more of them. They don't want you to be disappointed. Jake wanted to please his customer. If she was disappointed, she wouldn't come back to him in the future. Businesses – most of them anyway – will eventually go out of business if you're not happy!

And it's not just about the choices and quality of what we buy. It's about how much they cost. With capitalism, "competition" usually forces most businesses to price things as low as they can, while still making a profit. If they don't lower prices, more businesses will come in, at lower costs, and take their business away.

Millions of decisions in the marketplace occur every day because of a very simple thing – it's called "supply and demand." Supply means how much of a product is out there. This is one of the most important things about capitalism. Demand means how much people want it. Jake started fixing computers because he thought customers would have computer needs, which is high demand. He hoped there wouldn't be too many people who could fix computers as well as him – which means low supply. With high demand and low supply, Jake could charge customers enough money to stay in business.

We can go through hundreds of great examples of capitalism. At one time dishwashing machines, clothes washing/drying machines, automobiles, jets, air conditioners, and refrigerators did not exist. All of these things came to us through capitalism, making our lives easier and better. It seems magical, but it's not. It's just capitalism. In the end, capitalism changes the world through millions of businesses, one product and one sale at a time.

They Said It Long Ago...

Capitalism Helps Make Us Great - *"If businesses and people are free, they will find their way and become more productive. They will become far more productive than if even the best government tells them what to do!"*

—President and Founding Father James Madison
(paraphrased)

36

Jake's Customer Changes His Life

Remember that older lady who came into our shop just a few hours ago? Well, after she released me from a bone crushing hug, she introduced me to a very intriguing charity.

"Well, I'd better get back to my work. I have a truckload of food in the trunk of my car for the Brighton Center," she pushed her glasses up on her nose with her free hand.

At first, I was confused. What is she talking about? "Excuse me?" I asked. "What's the Brighton Center?"

"Oh, do you have a few free hours?" she asked wearily. I poked my head into the back of the store and told Jared to keep an eye on the shop.

"I do believe that my schedule has just been cleared," I told her happily. We exited the store and made the short walk to her cute yellow Volkswagen Bug. The drive to the charity was a little over fifteen minutes and along the way, she told me all about the work the volunteers do.

People who had nowhere else to go to get help came to the Brighton Center. As it turns out, the Center had lots of computers and people in the community doing job training on the PC's. She invited me down to meet the staff and the citizens who lived there.

The people at the Brighton Center had a strange sort of mood that made me feel pure and ready to lend a hand. The struggles of their clients, the stories of how the Center took care of people in need, caused me to think. Was I doing enough for our community? Did they need my help? Could they use my help? Well, of course they could. I started volunteering every week from 5:00-9:00 p.m.

Volunteering helped me realize just how fortunate I am. To think, I could've turned out like any one of them. And wouldn't I appreciate people's help? I planned to contribute to over a thousand volunteer hours and raise over $50,000 for the Brighton Center. I'm reluctant to tell you about it because we didn't do it to get attention. Several of our employees pitched in. We don't brag about doing it - we just did it. After all, volunteering is supposed to come from the bottom of your heart, not the top of the newspaper.

God blessed me and a lot of other people with talent and ability to help. We did it because it was the right thing to do. It brought us together as a business team. It made us grateful for what we have. In fact, I was even considering hiring a few of the more experienced people that we helped train at the Center. Who knew that helping others would help us too?

Capitalism Pointer - Charity Often Comes from Capitalism and Businesses

Part of being an American should be lending a helping hand to those in need. Charities all over the country help elderly, disabled and people in poverty. Who provides the money for these charities? If you look closely at most charities, a big, big part of their money comes from businesses, business owners, and successful business people. These individuals usually earn the most money and they often give the most away to charities.

We want everybody who works hard and smart to succeed. The next time you see a business person driving a fancy car, just keep in mind that this person may have given away many times the value of that car to charity. Many business people don't just donate money. Like Jake, they donate their time to help people in need.

Most business people keep secret how much they give. They don't usually want attention for just being good citizens. They think that donating their money is what they should be doing. The people who work for businesses are often also extremely generous. Their donations come from their earnings which come from business. Add it all up, and millions of people across the country get help because of businesses and generosity.

Many business people believe in pitching in and tackling problems together. People who believe in themselves and believe in their neighbors don't see problems. They see solutions. They believe they can accomplish anything they set their minds to do. Yes, charity and good deeds often come from businesses and capitalism.

Across the country, tens of thousands of children have toys at Christmas because of businesses. It's amazing they care so much about people, some of whom they've never even met! It's no wonder why communities with strong businesses are successful. We're all in it together, helping one another.

Smart business people understand that sometimes charities can help businesses just as much as businesses help charities. Every person is capable of greatness. Every person has talents and strengths. Capitalism doesn't work very well when people don't develop their talents and strengths. With capitalism, and millions of opportunities out there, we hope we can find the job opportunity meant for us.

But what happens when a person gets knocked down and can't seem to get up? He needs a helping hand, doesn't he? If we don't pick him up, he'll never develop his talents and strengths. Who should pick him up? Everybody, including neighbors, friends, churches, and charities!

Capitalism doesn't mean ignoring people who struggle. In this country, it usually means just the opposite. With capitalism, we rely on one another. We should help our neighbors. This is a big reason why business people give money to charities and donate their time. When we work together like this, everybody wins, including businesses.

Smart business people know they can't succeed if their employees and customers can't get up when they get knocked down. Most businesses like to be in communities which have a spirit of doing good deeds and helping people who need help. Through the jobs they offer and the charities they support, businesses become a big part of our communities.

They Said It Long Ago...

A Sense of Responsibility - "If you're in the luckiest one percent of humanity, you owe it to the rest of humanity to think about the other 99 percent."

—Business Leader Warren Buffett

With The Money To Help - "No one would remember the Good Samaritan if he'd only had good intentions; he had money as well."

—British Prime Minister Margaret Thatcher

America Is A Charitable Nation - "The work of volunteer groups...have helped make this the most compassionate, generous, and humane society that ever existed on the face of this earth."

—President Ronald Reagan

37

Adelaide Decides Where And How To Grow Her Business

The New York City store has been so successful that we've made enough money to open up five new stores. Instead of keeping the money we've made so far, I'm investing it in expanding the business. In what parts of the country will I open my very own boutiques?

Who has the lowest taxes? What about the best conditions? Well, it looks like I will be doing a lot of research before expanding. And then worries began to fog my thoughts. What if the stores fail? What if I have to close them because they aren't earning a profit? I shivered. I don't even want to think about that.

Isabella had called me just a few days ago, gushing about how well she and Jake were doing in Kentucky, which made me consider expanding to Kentucky. As long as the local and state governments don't interfere too much with Kentucky businesses, then that truly might be my next location. No offense, but I've worked too hard to get this far and then let the government take half of what I earn.

Anyhoo, I'm getting ready for the next big show – this one in Central Park in New York! It's open to the public to raise money for charity! I will never forget how much our family struggled before we came to America and after we got here. We hardly had enough money to buy the necessities, such as food and clothes. Now that I have money to expand the business, the least I can do is try to raise money for other people. And guess who's coming to the show?

A few days ago, Isabella called to catch up a little and I told her about my charity plans.

"That sounds awfully expensive, Addie. I'm worried that you will lose money for this show. If you want the money to go to charity, then get some other businesses involved to help you. More money would go the charities that way." Isabella always seemed to be a step ahead of everyone else and she definitely didn't fail to impress me this time.

I could hear the tapping of a pen on her wooden desk at work. "What if the runway was a milky white with little colors that flashed on and off to the beat of the music?"

"Okay, what's it made out of?"

"Umm…. Reinforced glass? Does that sound good? Glass always sounds good when heels hit it." I told her, sounding unnaturally snobby and fashionable.

I could feel her smiling through the phone. "Great. I can have that done by August for free."

"Bella, you really don't have to do that," I pleaded.

"Trust me, I want to. Whether its friendship, business or charity, we are always in this together. And I have another surprise for you," she informed me. My heart began to beat quickly. I loved surprises. They were just so…. Well, surprising! "Jake and I are coming to see the show!"

I think I must've heard her wrong. I'm officially homesick. I'm even putting words in Bella's mouth now! "What did you say?" I asked again.

"I said that Jake and I are coming to see the fashion show! Jake's software company is really hitting it off and people love it, so now we both have enough money to take a little time off and live it up with you for awhile in New York. We miss you! It's about time we got caught up, face-to-face" Isabella told me.

I was shocked. It will be great seeing Jake and Bella, and I missed them like crazy. I have been so busy with the business that I haven't taken time out to see my best friends.

"How long are you staying?" I asked, hoping it would be more than one day and one night.

I could tell that she hadn't really figured this part out yet when it took her a minute to reply. "I was thinking, since your show is on a Friday night, we could come on Friday afternoon and stay until Sunday afternoon. How does that sound?" I smiled to myself. Almost two whole days with them sounds perfect. I can't wait!

I heard someone knock on her office door and a voice from the other end. Isabella sighed and said something to the voice.

"Great, well I have to go. Smelting room emergency that needs attending to," she told me. She quickly bid me goodbye and the line went dead. I fell backwards on my expensive, plush comforter in my new state of the art four room apartment.

With a grunt, I pulled myself up and entered the room I used as my home office. The sketchpad sat face up, open on my desk. I clicked over to it, wearing my own heels, and began to design a new outfit.

I'm thinking that the theme of my charity show will be "Fall Picnic Under the Stars. Do you like it? If it goes as planned, we could raise over $100,000 for people who could get better use out of it than I could.

Capitalism Pointer – Reasonable Tax Rates Can Help Capitalism, Businesses and Jobs

As Adelaide decides where to open her next store, or where to locate the headquarters of her business, you can be sure she'll be looking at tax rates. People say that there are only two certain things about life – death and taxes. They're right. Very few people actually like taxes. But taxes are absolutely necessary for our government. We wouldn't have governments, fire or police protection without them. Adelaide should be willing to pay some of her earnings in taxes. But how much is too much?

The first mistake we can make would be to assume that Adelaide, Jake, and Isabella can automatically afford to pay high taxes. Most businesses don't make large amounts, when compared to their sales or the amount they spend or invest in their business. A great profit is around 5% of sales after paying your taxes. If a business owner works hard and sells a million dollars of its product, the owner could make about $50,000, for example, which is only 5% of sales.

Businesses consider many different factors when deciding where to locate and create jobs. Taxes can make a big difference in where jobs go, or whether they're created at all. The less a business earns and gets to keep, the less it has left over to expand and grow jobs. When a business looks at whether to expand or grow jobs, it needs to know that if the expansion will be worthwhile. If, for example, 50% of the new money made has to be paid in taxes, the expansion might not make much sense. On the other hand, if the business owner can keep more of the additional money earned through the expansion, she's more likely to expand and grow job. This is common sense, but for some reason many people don't understand it.

When people talk about taxes, remember, just about everything we do is taxed. When we buy something, when we make something, when we own something, even when we die, we pay taxes. There are federal taxes, state taxes, local taxes, retirement taxes, medical taxes. They add up. Almost everything you see in life, except for nature itself, is taxed at one point or another. If you own a business, depending on where it's located, you could be paying up to 50% of every extra dollar you earn in taxes.

It's true that many people in this country think business owners should pay more. But if business owners pay more, there will be less money for them to expand their businesses and create jobs. This is a simple arithmetic. If we know people who want and need jobs, or people who have jobs and want better jobs, we need businesses to do well. We might want to slow down and think about it before raising taxes on businesses and their owners.

In 2011, nearly 50% of Americans paid no federal income tax. These people typically earned lower amounts of money or no money. The top 1% of earners paid 36.3% of federal income taxes. The top 5% of earners paid nearly 60% of federal income taxes. The top 10% of earners paid over 70% of federal income taxes. Should they pay more? Even the people who want higher taxes must admit – business owners are already paying for most of our government!

If you believe it's fair to take 50% of every extra dollar a business owner earns, remember, that could affect all of us. Would you take every dollar you have and risk it on a business, knowing that if you succeed the government will take 50% of the additional money you earn? Many people won't take that deal. On the other hand, reasonable tax rates can help capitalism, businesses, jobs and all Americans.

They Said It Long Ago...

On Taking Taxes From Some To Give To Others - "Our country will cease to exist if our government takes from those who are willing to work and gives to those who do not work."
—President and Founding Father Thomas Jefferson
(paraphrased)

Stand Up Or Else – *"Supporting higher taxes for other people, but not yourself, is like hoping the crocodile will eat them first, but eventually, he'll get hungry and eat you too!"*

—President Ronald Reagan
(paraphrased)

38

Helping People In the Big Apple And Dreaming Of Making A Difference

Our jet landed in New York, also known as "the Big Apple." The crisp fall air hit our faces as we stepped off the plane. The air was chilly, but the forecast called for sunny skies and low seventies, so I expected it to warm up quickly as the day went on. Jake carried my suitcase off of the small Ultimate Air Shuttle jet as I began to get excited about my first trip to NYC.

We hitched a cab towards the hotel. Within a few minutes I could see the skyscrapers that shot above the low hanging fog. I understood why Adelaide loved this place so much. It was beautiful, that is, if you liked the hustle and bustle of big city life.

"Okay, so I'll meet you in twenty?" I confirmed. Jake nodded and we parted ways to our rooms. I quickly unpacked and called Adelaide to tell her we were here safely and would meet her in the dressing room in thirty minutes. I ran down to the lobby, impatiently clicking the elevator button. I couldn't wait to see Adelaide. I missed her like crazy and apparently, Jake did too because he was already in the lobby when I got down there.

"Ready to go?" he asked, bouncing on the balls of his feet.

"Of course!" We had a little trouble hailing a cab, but within five minutes, a yellow taxi pulled over and we gave him the address of the venue. He dropped us off in front of a building to the right of Central Park. There was a security guard standing at the doorway.

"Jake and Isabella? Adelaide's friends?" the guard asked.

"That would be us," I informed him. The guard let us in and pointed to a door marked 'green room.' I took a deep breath and flung the door open. The smell of hairspray and expensive perfume filled the air. "Hang back for a sec, Jake. This is a girl's dressing room. I'll get Addie to come out."

I looked around the large room, not exactly sure where to go first. I saw a long tunnel that was leading up to the runway on the edge of Central Park, so I decided to start there. I timidly walked down the tunnel, feeling oddly professional and out of place.

When I neared the end of the tunnel, I saw an older, more grownup version of the Adelaide that I once knew. Her hair was longer, legs taller, teeth whiter, eyes more angled. She looked like…. a model. She really did. If it wasn't for the professional pencil skirt and the clipboard in her hand, I would've mistaken her for one of the runway models. She turned away from the model that she was talking to and our eyes met. Her face lit up in a smile and she strutted over to give me a hug.

"How are you?" she asked in my ear. I squeezed her and then let go, leading her out of the tunnel.

"I'm doing great. I've missed you," I replied. "Jake is waiting outside the dressing room." When we reached the exit, Jake was standing literally right outside the door.

"Addie!" Jake yelled, hugging her tightly.

"How is the software company going?" she asked.

"It's great, really kicking off. People really like my new software and we're always trying to discover the next big thing," he told her. We spent the new few minutes catching up before Adelaide politely excused herself to go put the finishing touches on her masterpieces for the show.

Jake and I exited the building into the warm New York air. We entered Central Park and took our reserved seats in the third row. The trees swished in the wind and the sun beat down on the glass runway. I admired my handiwork and the way the light cast shadows of the green grass under the platform.

"It looks great, doesn't it?" Jake asked, leaning over to get a better view of the stage. I nodded and motioned to the stage, where Adelaide was stepping out. The glass reflected the sparkles that decorated her high heels as she stepped towards the front of the runway.

"Thank you all for coming to the very first presentation of my new line for Summer in Paris! I hope you all enjoy the summer outfits, which will be the first twenty. Then will come the fall sets, the last twenty. So sit back, relax and enjoy the show!" Addie boomed. She flashed the crowd an award winning smile and exited the stage, her hair ruffling in the slight breeze. The runway lights came on, the music was turned up, and thus, the show began.

And of course, her show was a huge hit! Everyone loved it. Even as the three of us sat in Addie's apartment, people came knocking. Some asked questions about her inspiration or past, while others simply wanted autographs and pictures. It was amazing.

When the clock struck 11:00 p.m., people started heading home and it was just the three of us. It was time to make my announcement. I hated keeping this secret from them, but I didn't want to tell anyone until we were all together. Plus, I had to be sure that this was the road I wanted to take. I guess it was time.

"Hey, guys," I whispered, interrupting a stupid argument about gummy bear flavors. Sometimes, they were such children. They turned their attention to me. "Well…. I've been thinking about this for a long time, and I was debating going into politics.

I'm only just getting started, but someday I'm hoping to run for governor of Kentucky."

It was a long time before they said anything. They all seemed to process the new information slowly, but surely.

"So that's why you have been away from your company so often lately! I wondered why you felt the sudden need to cancel our dinner last week!" Jake yelled, putting two and two together. I laughed at his realization.

"Do you really think you can win?" Addie asked.

This was a no brainer. "Not to be conceited here, but yes I do. All the people I'll be competing against are practically telling people they want to raise taxes. They have horrendous campaigns."

"They are practically begging for the government to control even more of our lives! Not one word has been said about new businesses that can potentially create new jobs. Yeah, yeah, yeah, they might be great speakers, which make their arguments sound believable, but anyone with a brain knows the real meaning behind their good speeches. If I'm elected, I want Kentucky to become the best place for businesses to thrive." I continued.

"If your plan works, there will be so many businesses that you won't have enough people to fill all of the jobs! Then more people will start to move to Kentucky. Am I right?" Addie confirmed, motioning wildly with her hands as if to prove her point.

"Yes! And I would just like to say that some of these people who run government don't know the first thing about the way to run a business! They have no idea that the only way to make sure people have decent jobs is to have so many jobs that employers have to pay the workers even more to get them, and then have to pay more to keep them. They have no idea that if everybody who wants a great job has one, that's our best tomorrow! My breathing was staggered and heavy as I finished my tirade.

They both snickered at my rant. "Thank you! It's nice to see that someone has some freaking sense! Taxes are so high and the government has so many stupid rules that it's getting next to impossible to start and grow a booming business. And if nobody can keep their businesses running, how will people get jobs? If you don't win, I think I'm going to die of horrible government." Jake fake died by dramatically falling onto the bed, messing up all the perfectly placed pillows and blankets. Addie, being the OCD fashion girl she is, hurried to fix the misplaced decorations.

"Don't worry. I will win, trust me."

Capitalism Pointer - Capitalism Can Help Build Good Citizens

You can see that Adelaide, Jake, and Isabella are becoming exceptional people. Somewhere in the history of your family, people did amazing things no one thought they could do. Maybe they came to America across an ocean in a crowded old ship, with barely enough to eat. Maybe they overcame discrimination or prejudice to get a job. Maybe they started a small business from scratch, or worked two jobs to help feed your ancestors! People who came here to seek a better life formed our country. "American exceptionalism" is all around us.

Our family has heroes of capitalism who helped us see America's greatness. Both of Lauren's grandfathers risked every penny they had on business ventures which they continue to own. They showed us how much a good job can mean to a family. They were good teachers, good citizens, and they were right. Lots of people did better in their lives because of the hard work of only two business people! Their children got college degrees and their children's children will get college degrees.

Capitalism helps build good citizens because it's about working hard and taking your best shot at life. It's about finding a path to do much better. Remember how you felt on your first job, with a job well done, or with a high grade on a test? We bet, pretty well. Remember how you felt when you were lazy or did poorly? We bet, probably not great. Most people know we are at our best when we're working and striving to get better.

The American dream is alive and well with tens of thousands of "unsung business heroes." They don't wear capes. They have no super powers. But every day, if we look closely, the example they set reminds us about good citizenship and American exceptionalism. They save money and risk it with their businesses. They hire people and help families.

Through hard work, having fun along the way, you will write your own success stories. You can write new ones, better than the ones before!

Chapter 39

While Isabella Thrives, Jake Struggles

For me, things in the business were going well, but in business things can change. I remember that night. It's funny how you always remember the details of an enormous catastrophe, but seem to forget the details of a mind blowing success.

I fell back into my plaid recliner, sighing as my eyes shifted around the living room in my very own house. A large flat screen TV sat in the front of the room, pressed against the far wall. Matching plaid sofas sat empty to the left of the recliner. The sound of the ceiling fan filled the heavy silence that echoed through my large house. Detailed cream colored molding lined the high ceilings, adding flair to the room.

Alright, well let's see, I was running a successful business. That in itself is already more than I expected. So I couldn't assume that it would stay like that forever. There are no guarantees that I'll keep doing well. Everything I've built and made in business could be lost with one mistake or bad decision.

Stop and Stare! I think I'm moving, but I don't- My phone sang the classic Nickelback song, filling the hollow peace. I quickly picked it up, cutting the song off mid-sentence.

"Hello?" I answered, running my hand through my short hair.

"Boss, we've got an issue," Jared, my assistant manager, informed me, his voice filled with worry.

What does it take to get a day off around here? I silently whined to myself. "What's the problem?" I asked, pursing my lips.

"A group of customers were doing tests of our software and they want to talk to you. Now." Jared said. I quickly jumped out of my chair and ran up the steps, thrashing into my room.

"Okay, I will be right over. Call everyone who's off duty and tell them to get over there. I will pay them extra," I told him, hanging up and tossing my phone onto the bed. I hastily pulled a pair of khakis over my plaid boxers and slipped a suit jacket over my white undershirt. I ran a comb through my hair, which didn't do much good. I buttoned the jacket with one hand as I slipped a black dress shoe over my left foot, then the right. I dashed out the front door, locking it behind me and hurriedly started my Acura.

I'm glad that my new office wasn't more than ten minutes from my house because by the time I got there, the representative of the group was mad as a hornet and very, very tired of waiting.

"Ahh, and you must be Mr. DiAngelo," he guessed, turning around to shake my hand. He was at least four inches taller than me, with jet black hair and an intimidating Spanish accent.

"Yes, sir I am, very nice to meet you…" I trailed off, not knowing his name.

He cleared his throat, dropping my hand. "Arthur Gregory, but you may call me Arty." He walked away without letting me have the chance to respond to his comment. He stepped towards the back of the store. "So, Jacob, when did your company invent this most recent piece of software?" he asked.

I struggled to remember how many years it has been. "About three years now I guess," I finally pinpointed.

"Three," he whispered to himself, scribbling something on his clipboard. "On average, how many units of your software do you sell a day?"

That was another hard question, but not as difficult to recall. "Well, we sell hundreds of copies each day."

"And do you allow buyers to download protection programs such as Norton?" he asked, pacing throughout the bright store.

"Actually, Arty," I felt my palms began to sweat. "I have pre-installed my very own protection program called Trak-it in every computer that we sell."

"You do, now?" he confirmed. I nodded my head. "May I test it?"

"Be my guest," I told him, leading him into the back office where my work computer sat.

"You," he yelled, pointing to Jared. "Bombard the computer with viruses." Jared complied, sitting down at a vacant computer in the store. I watched awkwardly as they both rapidly typed on their keyboards.

"So, I will just… leave you to it," I told Arthur, slowly stepping backwards out of the room. As soon as I was out, I shut the door behind me and sighed heavily. I had faith in my work, but nerves continued to pelt me. I ran my hand through my hair as the minutes ticked by to an hour. Finally, the door opened once more and out came an unhappy looking Arty.

"Mr. DiAngelo, I'm afraid there is a problem with your security software."

My heart sunk. These were the words that I had dreaded from the moment I decided to go into the software business. How could there be a problem? I checked and double checked and nothing that we had tried could get through. We missed this one though.

"What virus did you use?" I asked.

"It was a simple virus to hack into your email account. Easy peasy, but your software allowed the virus to get through," he answered, shrugging.

An awful feeling began to dwell in the pit of my stomach. I had failed, and, let me tell you, it felt horrible. I needed to fix the network, fix the software, and I needed to fix it quick. By the time we were done fixing it, thousands of customers had lost their computer systems and we ended up owing hundreds of thousands of dollars.

As the horridness of my mistake began to dawn on me, I had fallen into something that most people would call a "slump." I didn't have the energy to work, or sometimes, to even get out of bed. I had simply lost my motivation. But a simple call from Isabella changed my mind in a heartbeat. She believed in me, and if she did, then why shouldn't I?

I immediately began to work and work, not stopping until the issue was solved. As soon as I cracked the code, I tried to make sure every customer issue was addressed. Then, I got to work on our next product. One failure would not stop me from grasping heights that I never dreamt I would reach.

Enough about me, I forgot to tell you about Isabella. She was right. Again. She hired trustworthy people to manage her business and ran for Governor. But the most amazing thing about this scenario is that she inspired people across Kentucky to see how great we could be. She said that if we grow businesses and have more people employed, the government would have more money for safety and schools. All we need to do is make Kentucky the best place in the world to do business!

She won by a thousand miles. By a thousand miles, I mean the number of votes for her was so completely astonishing that next to nobody voted for her opponents. It was truly amazing! Isn't it strange how one leader can make a noticeable difference if people would just listen! I may be a bit biased here, but Bella is a great leader. She was a leader of a movement, a leader that lives to make a difference in the world.

Bella and I are getting closer and closer as a couple, (Yes, we are a couple. No, you are not allowed to laugh) but who knows what can happen? I'm still trying to run a business and she's leading the entire Kentucky government! Oh, what will I do with that girl?

Capitalism Pointer – "Growing The Pie" Is A Way For Everybody To Do Better

Jake mentioned something that Isabella did in Kentucky which worked. Most businesses like it when government gets more money by helping to grow more businesses, not by raising taxes higher and higher on the businesses we have now.

With more businesses, lower tax rates can actually increase money for the government. Here's how. With lower tax rates, more businesses may choose to invest and expand. They can make more money, pay taxes on the new money they make, and their new employees pay taxes. Business expansion can create new income, new jobs, new taxpayers, and more tax money for government, not less. Think of it as a delicious pie which gets bigger. The government gets a bigger slice because it's a bigger pie!

On the other hand, with high tax rates, a business might decide to hold on to its money instead of spending it to expand the business. Again, there's not as much incentive to expand and take risks if the government will take most of the new money made. When a business decides not to expand, it creates no new income and no new jobs. Nobody has new jobs which would have led to new taxes paid by new employees. Think of it as a lousy pie. The pie gets smaller and the government gets a smaller slice because it's a smaller pie!

It's this simple. If you want more tax dollars for government, would you rather have 1,000 new taxpayers paying $10 each in taxes ($10,000 in taxes) or only 10 taxpayers paying $100 in taxes ($1,000 in taxes). You'd rather have more taxpayers paying lower rates than a few taxpayers paying higher rates! The more our economy grows, the more taxes the government can collect. Everybody wins when that happens.

We know this is real. For example, some Presidents have cut taxes and the federal government actually collected more tax dollars. Later, the economy did poorly and the government collected fewer tax dollars. The pie got smaller, which meant less for everybody. This is fact, not fiction.

The amount of taxes collected to pay for our police, roads, bridges and government will always have more to do with whether the economy and businesses grow than it does with higher tax rates. That's why Isabella did what she could to grow, grow, grow! Many things can make an economy grow. Sometimes, fewer rules and lower taxes can make the pie grow larger so that everybody can win.

They Said It Long Ago...

On Growing the Pie - "There are no great limits to growth because there are no limits of human intelligence, imagination, and wonder."

—*President Ronald Reagan*

On High Taxes - "For a nation to tax itself into prosperity is like a man standing in a bucket and trying to lift himself up by the handle."

—*British Prime Minister Winston Churchill*

The Case For Reasonable Taxes - "Common sense told us that when you put a big tax on something, the people will produce less of it. So, we cut the people's tax rates, and the people produced more than ever before."

—*President Ronald Reagan*

40

Isabella's Big Chance To Change Her State

There was no time to waste when it came to changing things as Kentucky's governor. Governors who came before me have lived like kings and queens in the "Governor's Mansion" and they had a whole staff of people who waited on them hand and foot. It cost a fortune! As nice as all of that stuff sounds, I told them I didn't need it.

Alright, now I'd just like to say that the first thing I decided to do was really crazy. So crazy that thousands of angry people lined the street and the entrance to the Capitol building. Can you believe that it was only my first year as governor and I was already receiving hate mail? Some people are just so mean!

So I decided to dive into the world of labor unions. All of the Southern states had a "right to work" law, that is, except for Kentucky. With a right to work law, employees wouldn't have to pay union dues just to keep their job. Most businesses are crazy over the right to work because it's all about freedom and leading your own life. After all, shouldn't everyone have the right to decide whether to pay their money to a union? Yes, unions speak for many employees, but if you don't like them, then you shouldn't have to pay for them, right?

An old friend of mine, Dan, works at the Tri-County Economic Development Corporation. They talk to business owners and try to recruit them to Northern Kentucky. He told me that over twenty thousand people could have new jobs and better jobs if we had the "right to work" law. But with every good thing comes a down side. And the wicked witch of this situation was that the unions hated the right to work. The unions wanted people to be forced to pay money to them!

Instead of trying to calm the angry protestors, I took a stand. I took a stand for people to get more job opportunities. And I sure as heck wasn't going to be stopped by a few angry people holding signs up in my face and shouting at the Capitol building. I marched straight in there with my Jimmy Choo heels and told the legislature what I thought. I rushed to the ornate podium, slammed my hands on the wood, and looked them straight into their eyes.

Alright, maybe I didn't exactly do that, and I didn't exactly act like a brat, but I did tell them what I thought would be best for Kentucky.

> *It is a new day in Kentucky. We will no longer be a poor, small Southern state. We will no longer put the desires of a few people above opportunities for all people. We know that a Right to Work law will help us grow jobs. I will not stand by while graduating students want to work, but cannot find jobs. What about their rights? What about their opportunities? Shame on you for putting your union friends and old fashioned ways above the future of the young people in this state. I will fight for every person, young and old, who wants to work. I will fight for our best tomorrow. Will you join me?*

And guess what? My persuasive techniques led many of them to join me! Really, how could they say no to more jobs? Almost immediately after right to work became a new law of Kentucky, business after business started making plans to expand here.

With a few more helpful little pushes in the legislature, in the next few years it got even better. We reduced taxes for Kentucky and we made government smaller (with fewer rules, of course). Within four years, Kentucky had so many people wanting to do business that owners could hardly keep up! Everybody who wanted a job, and was more than willing to work for it, was hired in a heartbeat. The Bluegrass state became the envy of the nation.

With every growth step, there was ironic thing to top it all off like a cherry on a sundae. The more people who moved to Kentucky, the more taxes that were paid. The money paid to the government for our schools, roads and bridges just skyrocketed!

Capitalism Pointer – Unions and Business Owners Often Disagree

Unions "represent" employees where more than 50% of the employees in a workplace vote to have a union speak for them about their pay and jobs. When employers and unions sit down together and talk (it's called bargaining), at times they can find great solutions to workplace problems. Some unions also offer needed training to new workers. At one point in time during our nation's history, unions played a bigger part of eliminating inhumane and unsafe conditions in the workplace. Today though, unions represent less than 7% of company employees.

Most business owners and union leaders don't always agree. Wages for employees are usually set by the marketplace, which is to say somebody with valuable skills which are in demand usually gets paid more money. When a union asks that wages go higher and higher than the market (they want more money for an employee with low skills), and if the employer agrees, what happens if a competitor is paying lower wages and can lower its prices? This can put the employer with the union out of business.

If a union thinks the wages paid are too low, it can call a strike and employees walk off the job, which can put a business out of business. It's hard to see how anybody wins when this happens. Some unions also like complicated rules which make it difficult for companies to change when they need to change. This is one of the reasons why so few company employees are represented by unions. Over a period of time, their companies went out of business!

Unions have begun working with government employees. At times, government officials have provided very generous benefits to union workers and the union workers then campaign for the government officials to get re-elected. This might be good for the government worker, but it's not always very good for the rest of us. High benefits for government workers can increase the cost of government and make our taxes higher. As much as we want ourselves and government workers to do well, we need to be careful about high costs and high government debt. We're paying for government worker benefits and the strangest thing happens – their benefits are often better the ones we have for ourselves!

Unions, for some reason, don't usually favor pro-business candidates in elections. But one of the true themes of this book is that we should all root for one another to do well. Even though companies and unions often disagree, consider whether the best thing for a union would be to root for businesses to do better so that more employees can get more jobs and higher paying jobs. A business which does very well is in the best position to pay workers more! On the other hand, a company which goes out of business can't pay anyone anything.

Can you see how we really are all in this together? The sooner more people in our nation understand this, the better off we will all be!

They Said It Long Ago...

Unions Were Never Intended For Government - *"All government employees should realize that the process of collective bargaining, as usually understood, cannot be transplanted into the public service (where the people pay government worker wages through taxes)."*

—*President Franklin Roosevelt*

Working Together? - *"Absent management cooperation, the union movement will revert to the militant, confrontational mode of the '30s. We will use abrasive and confrontational tactics."*

—*Union Leader John Sweeney*

At Times, A Desire to Harm - *"Something historic is about to happen. You are about to see corporate America's worst nightmare come true."*

—*Union Leader Richard Trumka*

41

Adelaide Encourages Isabella To Go For It!

"Have you ever thought about doing more with your talents of leadership?" I asked Bella through the phone, twirling a pen in the hand. I tapped it on the desk, glancing out the window into the shop.

"Like what?" Isabella questioned.

I thought for a moment, dropping the pen. "I don't know. Maybe, like becoming the President!" I giggled, laughing at the thought of my best friend running the country's government. It's not that I didn't she was capable, but it just seemed weird that maybe someday the President could be a girl who had a huge part in me learning to speak the English language.

Isabella's role as a leader and her ideas were taking over the nation, even in my far away State of New York. Taxes in New York have never been low, especially in New York City. Our unemployment rate shot up in the last few years and to make matters worse, we have been losing businesses.

Don't expect me to start rolling in mud or working on a farm, but sometimes I actually wish New York was more like Kentucky! The government debt in New York is high and it's practically non-existent in Kentucky. Isabella's efforts to make government smaller and more efficient were huge successes.

I suddenly became worried as the other line grew silent. I could faintly hear the sound of the brunette's breathing through the phone. "Bella?" I asked.

"That's…That's an amazing idea, Addie! Oh, my gosh! We could change the country! Of course, you will be a big part of my campaign. That's an order, little missy," she told me. I could hear the ruffling of some papers and the typing of a keyboard on the other end. I assumed she was already trying to figure out how to become president.

Just then I saw a call coming in with a Kentucky area code. I quickly ended the conversation with Bella and took the call.

"Hello?" I questioned.

"Ms. Ballou? Hi, it's Angelica from your Kentucky store," she said. Her voice sounded worried and tired, as if she'd been up all night.

It took me a minute to match the name with the face of the sassy blonde running our Northern Kentucky location, right across the river from Cincinnati. "Ah yes, what's up, Angelica?" I asked, wondering why she would be calling me this late.

"Well," she began, sounding distressed. "We have a problem here in Kentucky. We can't keep enough good merchandise in the store. Everybody's buying it up. The economy is booming here and I was thinking that we should consider opening more Kentucky stores."

"Now, that's the kind of problem I like to hear Angelica! I'm coming to Kentucky and maybe, hopefully, I'll move the corporate headquarters and my office down there. I'm predicting that an old friend of mine down there will be President of the United States!"

Capitalism Pointer - Capitalism Can Make Better Jobs

Something amazing happened during Adelaide and Angelica's conversation. We just saw how businesses can make better and better jobs. Growth in Kentucky meant more high paying managers would be hired. If we have more jobs, pay and job benefits will go up, up, up! This happens because businesses have to pay more to get the best people to work for them.

Employee pay is another part of "supply and demand." When you have more jobs (demand) than you have people (supply), the price goes up! The price of workers is their wages and benefits. When we have the best place in the world to do business, employees get paid more and their families have more money! Capitalism does this.

Government rules on wages are the opposite of capitalism. What if, in the future, the government tried to dictate higher and higher wages? If a business couldn't afford the higher wage, the business wouldn't hire more employees. People would lose out on job opportunities, instead of getting their starts in the workplace. And what if the employer couldn't afford the higher wage for its current employees? It would have to fire them because of the government rule, even if the worker was doing a good job.

Generally speaking, supply and demand, not government rules, should determine what we get paid. If we have rarer, valuable skills which help a business to make money, we will get paid more. If we don't go to school and get no special skills, we aren't as valuable and we get paid less.

We get what we earn, which encourages us to go get more skills, which makes us better, smarter and stronger. This is America. Even though some people want to change it, our system has worked very well for many people for a very long time.

They Said It Long Ago...

Better Jobs - "America's abundance was created...by the productive genius of free men who pursued their own personal interests and the making of their own private fortunes. They did not starve people to pay for America's industrialization. They gave people better jobs, higher wages, and cheaper goods with every new machine they invented, with every scientific discovery or technological advance- and thus overall the country was moving forward and profiting, not suffering, every step of the way."

—Author Ayn Rand

42

Will It Be Lonely At The Top?

I waved my hand at the adoring crowd that filled the square just after I finished my acceptance speech. Today was the day that I was getting inaugurated.

"Isabella, Isabella!" People screamed from all directions. Cameras flashed rapidly from the hands of the paparazzi. Nobody wanted to miss the story about the first president coming out of Kentucky. They wanted the full details about how we plan to change the country as a whole.

Everyone wanted to meet me first hand. Everyone knew my name. I was famous. I was the President of the United States.

Just then light streamed in from the windows, startling me awake from my dream. I rubbed the sleep out of my eyes, trying to clear my head. I laid back down, trying to remember exactly what I had been feeling as the lights flashed and questions were screamed in my ears.

Adrenaline rushed through my veins, making me feel as if I could run a thousand miles. The smile on my face had been wide and true. It was…. Amazing.

To tell you the truth, running for President scares me a bit, and I had almost chickened out. The federal government has become so large that it's frightening. All I need to do is make the government more efficient by making it smaller. I need to make sure that we don't spend more tax dollars than we have. If I do something wrong, the blame will be all mine.

But will I be able to handle the pressure of the U.S on my shoulders? Can I do it alone - without someone standing by my side at even the toughest of times?

Capitalism Pointer - Questioning Government

Isabella said that making government smaller was a good thing. Government can make business success easier or harder, but true work success usually comes from us, one business and one achievement at a time. If success mostly comes from us, is it okay to question whether we need huge governments doing all the things they're doing?

Remember, its majority rule in this country. If the majority dislikes business, and if government has big power, then the majority can do things to put business out of business. The bigger and more powerful government becomes, it could do some good things, but it could also have more power to harm our freedoms, including the freedom to do business. Some people think this is controversial, but it's just common sense.

Government can literally take your earnings through taxes and give them, through benefit checks, to people who aren't working. This happens every day. It can prevent you from buying some things you want to buy or from selling things you want to sell. This also happens every day. Sometimes it can even prevent you from building on your property. This is common.

When these things happen, sometimes it makes sense and sometimes it doesn't. If a person has a disability which prevents them from working, it's understandable that they may get a government check which comes out of taxes you'll pay. If a product is dangerous, for example, it shouldn't be sold or bought. But when government has this much power, doesn't it make sense to at least question how far it can go? Sure it does.

Did Isabella, as Governor, do the right thing by not growing government and by not going into too much debt? Most businesses love it when the government manages money and tax dollars wisely. Managing money usually means making sure we're not spending more than we have. It also means paying close attention to the money spent to make sure it's not wasted. This is how most of us live our lives, but sometimes governments don't operate quite like wise people do in our own lives.

Should governments pay close attention to the dollars spent? Their money comes from us – the citizens and taxpayers. We elect the government and they take our money through taxes. Most people would agree that government should have a special duty to take care of our money and spend it wisely!

Why do some businesses care about big government spending and big government debt? Again, the answer is simple. When government spends too much money, sometimes it doesn't have money left to do the things it should be doing. When we run up high government debts, more of our taxes go to pay for the debt, not for things businesses and all of us need, which we can't do for ourselves – like good roads and bridges.

Businesses need good roads and bridges! Unfortunately, the federal government has stopped paying for most of our large bridges on national highways. Many parts of the country need new bridges and the federal government does not have the money to pay for them. They've spent the money on other things. The federal government has, at times, spent about twice as much on paying interest for government debt as they did on things like roads and bridges.

The crazy thing about this is that even after they spent all our tax money, they kept on spending. As citizens, we can't just spend as much money as we want to spend. We can't spend money we don't have! If we did, we'd be broke or out of business – there would be consequences. The government though is never homeless or out of business. The federal government has kept on borrowing money so it can keep on spending more money than it had. Many people wanted the government to borrow even more so it could spend even more. This is a fact, but is it an example of good government?

There are lots of reasons for high government debt. The government is trying to do more and more things for more and more people. In the past, people liked many of these things, so they re-elected the government. As much as some Americans may like this, it led to more government spending and a truly amazing list of things which tax dollars have been spent on – like video games, internet dating, poetry, television commercials, lizard crossings, and to study cow gas. It sounds silly, but it's true.

The federal government has grown so large and spends so much money that it's hard to even imagine what the amounts mean. Most families will never have a million dollars. The federal government spends over a million dollars every ten minutes. A thousand million dollars equal one billion. A billion dollars is so large that paying it back, one dollar every second, would take nearly 32 years. A thousand billion dollars equals only one trillion. Paying back a trillion dollars of debt, one dollar every second, would take about 32,000 years.

Our federal government has over 17 trillion dollars of debt. The more debt we run up, the more interest we will have to pay. Paying back 17 trillion dollars of debt, one dollar every second, would take over 500,000 years. Every baby born in this country now starts her life with a share of government debt of over $50,000. Not everybody agrees, but some business people think this is not responsible government. They think it's not fair to young people in our country – and they think that young people will be paying off our debts for quite awhile! What do you think?

They Said It Long Ago...

Too Much Power - *"A government big enough to give you everything you want is big enough to take away everything you have."*

—*President and Founding Father Thomas Jefferson*

Limited Government - *"Nations crumble from within when the citizenry asks of government those things which the citizenry might better provide for itself. ... [I] hope we have once again reminded people that man is not free unless government is limited."*

—*President Ronald Reagan*

Responsibility - *"It is incumbent on every generation to pay its own debts as it goes."*

—*Founding Father and President Thomas Jefferson*

Don't Pass On Troubles To Our Youth - *"A generous parent would have said, if there must be trouble, let it be in my day, so that my child may have peace."*

—*Thomas Paine, Common Sense*

Different Rules for Government? - *"People try to live within their income so they can afford to pay taxes to a government that can't live within its income."*

—*Author Robert Half*

43

Jake Fights Back And, As Always, Helps A Friend

The good news is that we fixed the bug in the system. The bad news is we had a really hard time getting back on our feet. Every magazine and news station covered the story of our broken security program and it drove customers straight out the door. Nobody would set foot near us for about three months and I was surprised that we didn't go out of business. We had to let some employees go in order to stay in business. It hurt me to see them go, but what choice did we have?

Just when I thought I was finished, done, out of business, we created a new shape and size for the average desktop computer and it sold like crazy! Everyone wants the newest thing, so that's exactly what I gave them. We became so busy that we opened new locations and hired more experienced workers. We were recruiting only the best and brightest and paying them the most.

Addie has settled quite well in Kentucky. She bought a nice house just a few blocks from Isabella's. Summer in Paris is so close to going worldwide and I can practically see her impatience. I know how much she would love to open a store in France. Through all of these years, she has never once forgotten her heritage. It would make her so happy to go back to show her home country what a success she has become.

I was spending most of my time with Adelaide today because Isabella is out on the road campaigning for President. When she first told me that she was running for president, I was on the fence about it. To be honest, it sounded crazy!

But then I remembered, we're talking about Isabella here. She had a good head on her shoulders and I knew that if she were to win, our country would be in good hands. She had already won her party's nomination and her only competition was the other party's nominee, Todd Yeel.

She seemed to be doing fairly well against such a strong competitor. But Todd Yeel's fatal mistake? He campaigned by telling people what he would give them as President. Isabella campaigned by telling people what they could earn, and how they could succeed in a better country if she became President.

I won't lie to you. Todd Yeel has run a dirty campaign occasionally. He has lied and said Isabella was a ruthless business person, when Isabella was actually providing people with jobs! And I'd also like to ask how someone can consider you ruthless when you gave 10% of your profits to charity?

Yeel said he wanted to take money from people who earned it and give it to other people, saying that it was unfair that some people had more and other people had less. Yeah sure, let's just forget about the people who put their sweat and blood into their jobs to earn that money.

I'll be honest here. A lot of people who want to have it the easy way want Yeel to be President. Isabella promised only one single thing- if people worked hard, they would have more opportunities to do better.

I made up my mind a long time ago. Even though I am a little biased, Isabella is obviously the better of the pair. That's why I've been out campaigning with Isabella from time-to-time, helping her get every vote she can. I believe in her as much, if not more, than I believe in this country. Todd Yeel likes government. But what he doesn't seem to like is businesses. Weird guy, isn't he?

On the other hand, Isabella kept talking about how much better all of us could do if businesses grew across the country. She inspired business people. We need the right leadership. No one can do that better than Bella.

Capitalism Pointer – Politics and National Spirit Can Help Capitalism, Jobs and Businesses

Isabella's message of hope and optimism can make a big difference. When you think about whether politics and national spirit affect capitalism, think about what happens in our everyday lives. People do better in places where they're wanted. People like to be in places where people care about them and want them to do well, where they know they will get help when they need it. Do business people feel the same way? Sure they do.

So what does it take to have healthy capitalism, businesses and jobs? Again, think of everyday life. Students usually do better with great teachers. Children tend to do well in great families. People have a better chance of doing well if they have opportunities. Businesses are just like people. In fact, they're owned by people and run by people. They react to what's going on around them just like the rest of us. They do better with encouragement and a healthy economy.

Picking on businesses won't help. Remember, business owners and business people didn't get where they are by winning the lottery. Often times they started out with less and worked more – like Isabella and Adelaide. They have to suffer through failures, like Jake.

When you hear people talk, listen for a couple of unfair criticisms. First, you may hear that business people don't care. That's a big lie. Most people care, including business people. Business people have a task to do. Their task helps the country. They take risks and grow their businesses, which usually results in jobs.

170

Second, you may hear that business people or pro-business politicians don't compromise. If compromise means passing only one, instead of two, new laws every year which make it more difficult to do business, then maybe they shouldn't be compromising! If we compromised every time like this, before long we wouldn't have as many healthy jobs and businesses left. Jobs would move to other countries! You can bet Isabella fought against this sort of compromise.

Once again, in America we are all in this together. One great example is the stock market. Nearly every American with a retirement fund has stocks in the stock market, where ownership shares of companies are traded. When businesses do better, stocks usually do better, and the retirement fund goes up, up and up. Some people think that only rich people own stocks and stocks don't matter in their lives. But really, that's not true. When businesses do better, most of us do better.

Our American politics and national spirit can help make this the greatest place in the world to do business. What if people across the country understood businesses? What if they understood the courage it takes for a new business person to risk it all to start a business? Voices like Isabella's help businesses to know that we root for everybody to do well, including them.

They Said It Long Ago...

We Should Act Like Winners - "Putting people first has always been America's secret weapon. It's the way we've kept the spirit of our revolution alive – a spirit that drives us to dream and dare, and take great risks for a greater good."

—President Ronald Reagan

44

America's Best Tomorrow

New York

"That's amazing, Bella! So you won Oklahoma?" I asked Isabella.

I could hear her beaming through the phone. "How many states have you won so far?" I asked.

For a moment, there was no sound. Isabella then announced "I have won thirteen out of twenty-one so far!" If we were together now, this would be the time where I would pick her up and spin her around. But since she's not, I smiled like an idiot at the phone. I wonder if I will get to visit the White House when she wins! It's always been a dream of mine to visit the White House!

"Bella, that's great! You're doing great! I know you'll win!"

Campaign Headquarters in Northern Kentucky

My head was pounding and my heart was thrashing inside of my chest. I knew the cameras were on me, so I tried to keep my cool. I stared straight into the camera as the news counted the votes. Meanwhile, Todd Yeel looked at the cameras and smirked. He was so cocky! One day, that arrogance is going to come back to bite him. He thinks he can become President by simply promising everybody everything. That's not the way our country works!

I've told the truth. Win or lose, I wouldn't have changed anything. I watched as the cameras pan over to my face again, as I tried to put on an award winning smile. Even though I felt like I was hyper-ventilating inside, I knew that I couldn't show emotion. I better get used to keeping my emotions inside because the first rule of being President is "never let 'em see you sweat." A man with a microphone rushed up to me.

"What are you feeling right now, Ms. Waters?" he asked, shoving the microphone in my face.

I calmly took it from him. "I'm feeling pretty good about my chances. I'm also feeling pretty confident in America's chances of a rebirth." He smiled at me and then the television coverage switched over to an interview with Yeel.

"What about you, Mr. Yeel?"

His face exuded confidence. "I am actually feeling incredible," he answered simply. His short answer made me even more nervous. How was he so confident? Wasn't he at all nervous? I knew the answer to that. Of course he wasn't.

Maybe he didn't believe that he could be beaten by a woman, especially one coming out of Kentucky. Well, I'll show him. Women can do anything a man can and, trust me, sometimes we even do it better.

Calm down. Calm down. You've got this. I told myself. The television announcer looked up from his papers and turned to several people just in the camera frame. Oh, gosh, were they done? My heart pounded and butterflies fluttered in my stomach. One man stood up and walked over to the podium.

"America's votes have been counted tonight and our country has come to a conclusion," he boomed. I closed my eyes, crossing my fingers.

This is it. My thoughts traveled to my childhood, how my dad passed away and how my Mom struggled every day. The loneliness that ate away at me until I met Jake and Addie. All the hard nights spent in the dorm at college studying until 3:00 a.m. Working at Toyota during the day and trying to start my company at night.

My mind raced to the better parts of my life. Finally opening the business, all the jobs we created, how we changed Kentucky, and most of all, having my two best friends right by my side, supporting me the whole way.

All of that hard work seemed to come down to this moment. Could an unpopular, poor girl who was once friendless and seemingly had no future, run our country?

The announcer took a deep breath, "Our next President, Ms. Isabella Waters!"

The confetti and celebration began. It was then I realized I wouldn't be doing this alone. My new fiancé` gave me a big bear hug. I cherished the moment away from the crowd, away from the cheers, away from the screams. It was a moment, frozen in time, shared with the one who had always been there; the one who had been right for me all along.

Not even a year later, Jake and I had a white wedding, in the White House. Addie was there, crying and wiping her eyes with a handkerchief from the coat pocket of her steady boyfriend of four months. Together, never apart, we grew jobs and expanded the economy. And just like in the fairytales, we lived happily ever after.

Final Capitalism Pointer – Why Did Isabella Win?

Isabella followed the ideas on which we founded America - government having a few powers, with us having great freedoms. Not everybody agrees with this approach. But freedom means living in a place where the government is not always telling people and businesses what they can and cannot do.

We set up this form of government to inspire individual achievement and success. It's up to us to work hard and smart to succeed. On "Independence Day," July 4, we celebrate freedom

174

from the tyranny and oppression of English government. We celebrate our "independence" to be free people.

Just as adults are independent of their parents, we should be independent and free from unreasonable government control or involvement in our lives. You might say that, as Americans, we are not children and the government is not our mother or father.

We built this country from scratch. It didn't happen by itself. Great men and women strived to achieve more and more. The freedom of capitalism, businesses, and people has been a big part of our success.

While other countries tried other forms of government like socialism and communism, our form of "limited" government helped us become one of the most prosperous nations in history. With free markets and capitalism, we had ups and downs, but most people had jobs.

We had millions of people doing their best, with the incentive of earning more for their families, which made it all happen. With millions of people pursuing the American dream, we succeeded.

Todd Yeel's ideas are a bit like other forms of government which America did not choose – communism and socialism. As Jake explained, Mr. Yeel wants the government to take from some people and use that money to give things for free to other people. At first, it sounds good when somebody says you can have things for free. But in the long run it often doesn't work very well.

Why would you work hard and get a great education and a great job if you would make the same money as someone who didn't? Most of us would be lazy and that would eventually hurt the entire country. People with great ideas to make money and improve lives wouldn't have as much incentive to go into business and hire people. Why would they – if the government is just going to take most of what they earn and give it away to other people for free? With more and more people sitting on the sidelines of life instead of getting in the game, we all lose.

175

Capitalism means believing in ourselves and others. No matter how hard they try, governments can never guarantee good lives in the long run. A government check for someone who has the ability to work is never as good as a great job. We're responsible for our own success and happiness.

In your life you will have many choices. Don't shortchange yourself by falling for promises which at first seem good, but which are really like socialism or communism. If it sounds too good and too easy to be true, then it's probably false. Isabella spoke up for what she believed in. Enough people listened and she inspired them to do better, which is why she won!

They Said It Long Ago...

Equal Misery - "Socialism is a philosophy of failure, the creed of ignorance, and the gospel of envy. Its inherent virtue is the equal sharing of misery."
—British Prime Minister Winston Churchill

Less Government Can Be Better - "We are learning that the way to prosperity is not more bureaucracy and redistribution of wealth but less government and more freedom for the entrepreneur and for the creativity of the individual."
—President Ronald Reagan

Socialism - "Socialists cry 'Power to the people,' and raise the clenched fist as they say it. We all know what they really mean—power over people, power to the State."
—British Prime Minister Margaret Thatcher.

Big Government Cannot Do Everything - "I predict future happiness for Americans if they can prevent the government from wasting the labors of the people under the pretense of taking care of them."
—Founding Father and President Thomas Jefferson

No Free Lunch - "Pennies don't fall from heaven – they have to be earned here on earth."
—British Prime Minister Margaret Thatcher

And A Joke About Government - "If you put our federal government completely in charge of a desert, in that desert, in five years, there would be a shortage of sand."
—Milton Friedman, Economist (paraphrased)

Part Five
Get Your Game On!

45

Be Honest And Stand Up For What's Right

People in our country have big differences and one part of helping people is being honest about our differences. Some people think government can solve most problems. They want the government to do more. Other people believe more in themselves, their friends and neighbors. They want the government to do less. People will never agree on everything. But we can come closer to agreeing on something as simple as this - better businesses and better jobs help families.

People who think the government can solve most problems will keep saying we need more government solutions. Most people like compromise, peace and harmony. You may someday feel pressure to accept compromises even if you don't agree with them. It's okay to resist compromise when you know it's the wrong thing to do in the long run for businesses and families who need jobs.

We should respect people who choose to stand up for what they believe in. Wouldn't we respect them in other parts of life? We would say they are strong, determined, and honorable. Why should it be any different in politics or business? Stand up for what you believe in. We need you to help make our country great.

What are some good principles to believe in with capitalism, businesses and jobs? Business groups often adopt principles, such as favoring reduced taxes, reduced business regulation, and reduced costs of doing business. Most business groups favor international trade, management rights and capitalism. Not everybody agrees, but most business people think these principles can help businesses grow, which helps provide jobs for families.

What happens when you speak out on these things? Sadly, at times people will say you don't care about others. That's not true. Of course, you want people to do well, but you may believe in a different path to get there. Strong businesses make good jobs and wages for as many people as possible. Other people may want more government rules, but more rules may not produce good jobs and wages in the long run.

Focus on communicating how your approach will improve people's lives. Remember, anybody who speaks the truth takes risks. That's just life. The good news is that if you stand up for what's right, you'll respect yourself and you'll earn respect from others. In the end, they might even agree with you!

They Said It Long Ago...

Standing Up - "You have enemies? Good. That means you've stood up for something, sometime in your life."
—British Prime Minister Winston Churchill

Principles Are Important - "If we value what we get from government more than our principles, we'll soon lose both."
—President Dwight D. Eisenhower (paraphrased)

We Can't Always Agree – "To me, consensus seems to be the process of abandoning all beliefs, principles, values and policies. So it is something in which no one believes and to which no one objects."
—British Prime Minister Margaret Thatcher

46

Get Involved
With Friends and
Business Groups

The strength of a community can come from its people, businesses and business groups, such as the Chambers of Commerce. Chambers of Commerce help communities with economic development. They give advice to businesses, help them with training, and welcome businesses to a community. If you're going to be in business you are going to need friends. Businesses can usually find plenty of them at Chambers of Commerce.

Businesses pay for Chambers of Commerce and the businesses receive help because everybody can work together to help people get good job opportunities. Chambers of Commerce and other organizations which serve businesses are an important part of capitalism. If you get involved with business groups, chances are you're going to enjoy it. The people who participate want to help businesses and help other people. It's a big part of how we form a "community."

In our part of the country, we have local businesses and we have a regional business group called the Northern Kentucky Chamber of Commerce. If you attend a meeting there you'll find scores of people who just want to do the right thing. In some ways, over 300,000 people in our area depend on the Chamber to help people get and keep great jobs. It's a privilege to be involved in a group like this.

The future is in your hands, even if you don't think of it that way. It's great when we believe in America so much that we spread the word, sometimes one person at a time or one group at a time. To be the greatest person you can be, you'll want and need friends, including those you meet through business groups.

They Said It Long Ago...

The Importance of Friends - "A true friend advises justly, assists readily, adventures boldly, acts patiently, and defends courageously."

> —William Penn
> Founder Of Pennsylvania
> (paraphrased)

Speaking Your Mind - "A friend is a person with whom I may be sincere. Before him, I may think aloud."

> —Ralph Waldo Emerson
> Philosopher, Poet, Author

Something in Common - "Friendship is born at that moment when one person says to another: 'What! You, too? I thought I was the only one.'"

> —C.S. Lewis
> Writer, Theologian, Scholar

47

Encourage Smart Debate, Find Allies, and Make Partners

Isn't it great when everybody agrees on something and there's no need to even discuss it? What if it keeps happening over and over again? That would be great, right? Maybe not. When you don't debate or discuss things, you stop learning from others and sometimes you don't make the best decisions.

Polite, respectful debate helps us all. In this book we've covered different things relating to capitalism, businesses, and jobs which need to be talked about. If you don't speak up, there's a good chance no one will, which means others won't understand capitalism.

As you learn more and talk/debate with others, you'll be able to do a better job of figuring out what's right and wrong. Someone who wants your vote someday might deliver a nice speech. But do their ideas make sense in the long run? A candidate might look like us or talk like us, but will their ideas really work in the long run? They might even look or act like a rock star, but do they really understand capitalism? It's important that they do!

You probably wouldn't even buy a concert ticket without knowing the band's music. Casting a vote for President is much more important than attending a concert. Take a look at their websites and read up on candidates. Take pride in the fact that you're an American who pays attention to our country's future.

What about working together? Even if you don't agree on everything, if you agree on a business issue, work together! If you're a Republican, work with Democrats on pro-business issues. If you're a Democrat, work with Republicans on pro-business issues. Many business people care more about the issues than they do about political parties. It's about doing the right things to help the country overall, in the long run.

What about voting? When you're trying to figure out which candidate to vote for, you probably won't find the perfect candidate. Opportunities make such a big difference in people's lives. Consider whether the candidate understands capitalism, businesses and jobs. This will be important part of whether they can do the right things to help or hurt jobs in the long run.

48

Understand Media Bias

Some schools don't teach very much about capitalism. Where will Americans get their information? They could get information from family members, but not all families understand or talk about businesses. They could get information from friends or in their workplaces, but maybe not enough.

The only thing left is the "media," which is where we're supposed to get much of our news and information. The "media" includes television, newspapers, on-line services, and just about anything which sends messages and information to us. Members of the media include those who gather news and information and those who pass it on to us.

The media could do a great job of explaining businesses to us. However, most members of the media have never run a business or gone to business school. Some members of the media don't understand very much about capitalism. Just because they're members of the media doesn't mean they know what they're talking or writing about. They're only human.

We don't hear many media reports praising businesses and job creation. We don't hear many reports talking about high taxes, high debt, or over-regulation. We hear many reports which are just the opposite.

The truth is, media "bias" for and against capitalism exists. Bias is when a media member presents only one side of the story – the side which they like. The media also can try to entertain us, without presenting the full truth. These approaches aren't very helpful. They're downright frustrating when you're trying to figure out what's right.

A lot of what you will see and hear in media news is a "debate" or discussion among people with different views. You can learn from these debates, but remember, not all views are correct. Someone who looks good or sounds good may not be making any sense at all.

With the media, you'll need to reach conclusions on your own. It's not always easy, but it's one of the most important things we do as Americans.

They Said It Long Ago...

We Can't Correct What We Don't Understand - "Whenever the people are well informed, they can be trusted with their own government. If well informed, when government goes wrong they will notice and set it right."
—Founder and President Thomas Jefferson
(paraphrased)

The Truth Sets Us Free - "The spreading of true information is the only thing which really protects our freedom."
—Founder and President James Madison
(paraphrased)

49

Be A Student of History

You can be very effective for businesses and jobs by taking some time to learn what things worked and what things didn't work for capitalism in the past.

President Ronald Reagan took office with very high 12 percent inflation, very high interest rates at 16 percent, and very high unemployment. Our nation had low morale at the time. President Reagan helped lead the nation to its longest period of peace-time economic expansion.

Within a year after the federal government passed tax cuts, the economy started turning around – slowly at first, but much faster later. President Reagan, a Republican, and House Speaker Tip O'Neil, a Democrat, worked together for the good of the country. Although the federal government went into debt, the debt was way, way below the debt we have today. Democrats and Republicans saw the benefits of a strong economy.

President Reagan frequently praised capitalism and businesses. He spoke out against excessive government rules. You have seen many of his quotes in this book. Not all people liked what President Reagan and Tip O'Neil did. But their approach worked. They inspired business confidence.

Businesses felt comfortable taking chances and growing, which is exactly what they did!

It's not about blame, popularity, liking or disliking someone, getting mad, or getting even. It's all about what works for families who need our country to get it right. History can teach us a lot.

They Said It Long Ago...

Common Sense - "My policies are based not on some economics theory, but on things I and millions like me were brought up with: an honest day's work for an honest day's pay; live within your means; put back a nest egg for a rainy day; pay your bills on time..."
—British Prime Minister Margaret Thatcher

About History - "The farther backward you can look at history, the farther forward you are likely to see."
—British Prime Minister Winston Churchill

History Teaches Us - "My reading of history convinces me that most bad government results from too much government."
—President and Founding Father Thomas Jefferson

50

30 Common Sense Capitalism and Business Tips

Because we communicated ideas in different parts of this book, we thought it might be helpful to provide a summary, and some additional tips to consider about capitalism and government.

1. Capitalism Is Simple - Everybody can understand the basics. You can help teach other people and make the difference. Generally, when we do things which encourage business growth we have more, better jobs. When we place lots of restrictions on business, we increase their products/services cost and they may not do as well.

2. Stand Up For Growth and Jobs - If you oppose a new rule which sounds good but which could hurt businesses and jobs, you might get criticized, but that's okay. Standing up for what's right isn't always easy, but they say people who stand for nothing will fall for everything!

3. Live The American Dream – A big part of the American dream is work, success and achievement. We do the best we can to help ourselves and to help others. Hard work

and achievement develop your character and ability to help others. If you make good choices, others will see you as a role model. You can help them reach their own American dream.

4. Keep Learning – Learning more gives you confidence. Also, find business groups and people who will help you. They keep us inspired!

5. Know Some History - Pay attention to what seemed to work and what didn't seem to work with capitalism, businesses, and jobs. When we understand good history, we can learn from it and do better. If we don't understand bad history, we're doomed to repeat it.

6. Take A Positive Approach - People who understand capitalism and businesses are often looking out for everybody in the community. People like this want more jobs that help everyone.

7. Big Government – Families, neighbors, communities, churches, and charities do a great job of helping. Their help is voluntary and usually person-to-person. If we rely just on large governments to help all people, we can miss out on opportunities to connect with other people in very meaningful ways.

8. It's Okay To Disagree – Most people want to agree with other people. But should you agree with someone if they want you to do something wrong? Of course not. It's okay to disagree with a new rule or a new tax for business owners which may not work in the long run. People should hear both sides of the story!

9. Compromise Is Not Always Good - It's often okay not to compromise. If we were in a football game and I said, let's start at the 50 yard line, you would think that was fair. That's in the middle of the field. But if I ask you for 20 more yards and you give me 10, I'm now at your 40 yard line. If I ask you for 30 and you give me 15 more, I'm at your 25 yard line. Pretty soon I'll be in the "red

zone" running in for a score against you. You're a great compromiser, but you just lost the game. Be careful of compromises – at least when they mean compromising our rights or our future.

10. Be Patient - You won't always win. Nobody does. Sometimes it takes years to succeed, and sometimes it takes awhile for people to see you had a good idea. That's what happens when you lead – you're out in front! When you succeed, celebrate!

11. Economics Is For Everybody - Economics and job creation should be for all Americans. These things shouldn't be about Republican or Democrat politics. They should be about the right things to grow businesses and jobs to help all Americans.

12. Too Many Rules - Most new government rules sound good, but too many of them can hurt in the long run.

13. When They Say It Can't Be Done – They're probably wrong. We can accomplish anything economically in America, particularly if we can create the best business climate in the world.

14. Don't Trash Talk - You succeed by looking for ways to agree on business issues and going forward positively.

15. Defend Businesses At Times – No part of our country is perfect. But if people, the media, or an elected official criticizes regular business things like trying to make a profit, it's okay to speak up. If we don't, people may never learn the truth.

16. Government By The People - The government really has no money without the jobs grown by business and the taxes which businesses and their employees pay.

17. Root for Everybody - We appreciate wealthy people who buy things because when they do, somebody has a job producing the things they buy. We appreciate business owners who risk what they have and succeed, which leads to jobs for us. In America, we should want everybody to do well.

18. **Remember How We Get Better Jobs** – A great way to start a strong middle class is to grow more and more jobs. That way when we graduate college or go out to work we'll all do better.

19. **Business Growth and Jobs Can Help Everybody** - One of the best ways to strengthen families is through a good job in a strong economy. Children and families in homes doing well often do better.

20. **Remember Supply and Demand** – The price and availability of things and services mostly occur because of supply and demand. If people want something, then others will supply it in the economy. This is because so many people are trying to get in business and stay in business. New ideas and new products come out all the time because businesses believe people will want to buy them. Some of the ideas help everybody!

21. **Identify Principles and Try To Stick To Them** - Through this book and other life experiences, you'll identify principles. Make a list and try to stick to them.

22. **Good Government** - Investing in things like water, sewer and transportation infrastructure can help with business expansion and commerce. We need good government to do these things because none of us can go out and do them for ourselves.

23. **Not So Good Government** - Paying people for a little while to buy cars, golf carts, and other items (which our country has done at times) does not do that much good. When government tries to do too many things which we should be doing for ourselves, this can be a problem.

24. **Huge Debts** – Some debt is part of life. We may go into debt for a house or a great business idea. But when governments run up huge debts, they struggle to do the regular things they should be doing. Some day the debt will need to be paid off.

25. Businesses Create Jobs - Businesses have a lot of pressure to spend their money wisely, or they'll lose their own money. They're usually run by smart people with good ideas on how to make profits and to grow. Governments have lots of smart people, but they don't really grow jobs and they don't really have exactly the same incentives as us to spend money wisely. Government can do great things. Good government creates things like good bridges, roads, water, etc. But in the end, it's up to us to create the businesses and jobs.

26. Businesses Create Wealth - When a business expands, it typically seeks a modest profit (5% or so after taxes), but the government and community can benefit from the business much, much more than the business itself. Employees benefit. Governments benefit. The business owner puts her own money at risk. We think she has earned and deserves our respect.

27. Competitiveness – Businesses compete against businesses all over the world – and sometimes we lose! Losing can mean closing the doors of the business and firing all the employees. If one state raises taxes too high or puts in harsh business rules, then a business may need to move to another state to stay in business and compete. If our country raises taxes too high or puts in harsh business rules, then a business may need to move to another country to stay in business and compete. When people talk about higher taxes or more business restrictions, think about whether the taxes or rules will help us compete. If we aren't competitive, we will lose jobs. That's a fact.

28. Fairness - Is it "fair" to make a business owner who started out with less, worked harder, and risked everything, pay a high income tax rate of 40%? Is it "fair" that a person who started out with more, worked less, and risked nothing, should pay a low rate of only 5%? For some reason, most people believe this is fair, and that's what it's like in our country, but isn't it worth thinking about? Fairness can be a tricky thing – the person who worked hard might think it's unfair, while the person who didn't might think it's fair – and might even want the hard worker to pay more!

29. Slow Down And Consider All The Angles - Don't be too quick to take away the rights of a business owner. Even if it sounds like a good thing to do, they own their business, not us.

30. Be Optimistic – Have faith in our country, even though we're not perfect. Have faith in yourself.

51

Answer These 50 Questions To Become The Expert!

Okay, you've done the "heavy lifting." You probably enjoyed reading Lauren's portions of the book about Adelaide, Jake and Isabella. We hope you also read the capitalism pointer sections. If so, you have already begun to see our country, capitalism, and businesses differently. By spending just a few minutes thinking through the questions below, you will never forget what you've learned.

1. Capitalism is striving to own a business in the hopes of making a profit. As a result of capitalism, people have job opportunities. Why should people learn about capitalism?
2. With capitalism, you can start with nothing and reach for the American dream. Is capitalism just for rich people, or is it for everyone? It's for everyone, why?
3. With capitalism, all Americans can have hope for their best tomorrow. People can do better. One very successful business can improve thousands of lives. How can capitalism have such a large impact on people's lives?
4. Where do we get our money? Where does the government get its money?

5. Without capitalism, could we build great cities or great education? What would be the best way to get more money for education?

6. What would happen to our cities and education if capitalism, businesses and jobs started doing very poorly? Why?

7. Without capitalism, we would not have as many choices in the marketplace. Competing businesses are constantly striving to sell us goods and services. They're always trying to come up with the next new idea. What would life be like without capitalism?

8. How does supply and demand work? How does it affect the price and quality of what we buy?

9. If we have a starter job paying a low amount of money, capitalism can produce new job opportunities for us. Is there a limit to how good things can get if more and more businesses want to be in America?

10. Should the government want to try to help make America the best place in the world to do business? Why?

11. Capitalism is part of our American spirit. We've built great things in this country. We've accomplished great things. What are some of the different parts of the American spirit which are credited to capitalism?

12. Business people and business owners donate money and time to charity and do good deeds in communities. Why do you think they do this?

13. Capitalism can help build good citizens? What are the success stories in your family? What did capitalism have to do with these success stories?

14. The idea with capitalism is that if we build and grow enough businesses, then everybody will do better. Is it okay to root for a wealthy person? Why should we all root for one another?

15. Do you think most people understand what capitalism does for our country? If not, why not?

16. Will you choose to speak up and help make America the best place to do business in the world? Is this something which is worth your time and effort? Why or why not?

17. Governments have a special duty to spend our tax dollars wisely. Most state and local governments must balance their budgets and they cannot spend more than they have. Should the federal government be required to do this? If not, why not?

18. What is the proper role of government? Should they try to do everything, or only those things which we, as people, can't possibly do on our own? What are the things the federal government should be doing?

19. Businesses need the federal government to handle things like bridges and roads. What are the dangers of the federal government spending more money than it has?

20. The federal government has over $17 trillion in debt. Who will be paying this debt?

21. What if we behaved like the federal government in our own lives when it comes to spending? What are the problems with spending more than you have to spend in our personal lives?

22. Should the federal government spend money to pay for people's healthcare and for their retirements? If not, why not?

23. What are your thoughts about the federal government running up over $50,000 in new debt over the last several years for every person in America, including you?

24. We need to pay taxes to have government. What do you believe is a reasonable total amount for us to pay as a percentage of our income to all the governments, including local, state, federal governments?

25. Businesses usually make only about 5% after paying their bills and their taxes. How can higher taxes can affect whether a business grows?

26. What is the best way to raise tax money for the government? To grow the pie larger so the government and all of us can have larger slices, or for government to just take a larger piece of the same size pie or a smaller pie?

27. In the past, the federal government collected more taxes than it had ever collected before, and it had lower tax rates. How did that happen?

28. Is it fair for people with higher income to pay higher percentage tax rates? If rates are equal, like 20%, and they earn five times more, then they will pay five times more in taxes. Many people say it's fair for higher income people to pay an even higher rate, like 40%, than lower income people. What do you think?

29. In some years, nearly 50% of all Americans have paid no federal income tax. The top 10% of the country has paid over 70% of our federal income taxes? Is this fair?

30. A big key to tax rates are whether they are competitive. If you fought for higher tax rates because you thought it was fair for rich people to pay more, but then one of your friends lost his job because his employer decided to move to another state for lower taxes, how would you explain your stance to your friend who just lost their job? Would you blame the employer for moving?

31. Can you list four items to consider when thinking about government rules?

32. Many rules have nice sounding names and help some people. Can rules slow businesses and job creation down? How?

33. Why do you think we're unable to remove very many government rules, but we keep passing more?

34. Should we treat businesses like we treat our neighbors or friends? Why or why not?

35. We all want things to be more safe. But if more and more rules make our sewers, water and power more and more expensive, can this go too far? If so, why?

36. What kinds of problems for businesses can be caused by employees suing their employers in cases which have no merit?

37. Communism involves government control of wages and basically providing people with the same wages even if they do different jobs with different values. Why does communism sound so good to some people?

38. With communism we remove the incentive for people to work hard and do well. When that happens, eventually the system can fall apart. Name two things which America could do which would be like communism?

39. With socialism, the government takes over industries. If the government promises to take over an industry and make it work well, this would sound good to many people. What is the downside of socialism?

40. What are the things our country is doing, if any, which are similar to socialism? What about when the government takes taxpayer dollars and invests them in one business, but not another business? What is the downside of this?

41. Low interest rates and low inflation can help capitalism. What are the dangers of high inflation and high interest rates?

42. International business and competition can hurt American businesses when foreign countries become so attractive that our jobs move there. But international business helps our country in several ways. How does it help?

43. Do you believe the media reports on capitalism accurately? How could our education system do a better job of teaching capitalism, businesses and jobs?

44. How are religion, morals and charity connected with capitalism?

45. What would you think if you tried to start a business but people in the country and your elected officials said and did things which were against businesses? How do our national spirit and politics affect capitalism?

46. Should we be against people with more money or should we root for them? Is capitalism a way to bring Americans together or does it divide people?
47. How would you get involved in fighting for capitalism, businesses and jobs?
48. What would your principles be when it comes to capitalism, businesses and jobs?
49. Do you think debate and discussion is a good thing? How does it help?
50. Do you believe we can have our best tomorrow and a brighter future with stronger capitalism, jobs and businesses?

52

Choose
Your Future

You can make a powerful choice. You can be part of one of the most important decisions we make as a country. We can choose to make America the best place in the world for capitalism, businesses, and jobs. If we do this, we can help change lives for the better.

Don't underestimate yourself. You can help your country. In your life you will have many opportunities to say what you mean and mean what you say. You can be heard. You can make a difference.

What path will you choose? Will you speak up for America's jobs and businesses? Will you teach others? If you do, you'll be helping all Americans, whether they know it or not.

Part of fighting for capitalism, businesses and jobs is having the ability to see our best tomorrow and to be optimistic about it. Imagine what will happen if all Americans decide they like businesses and capitalism. More people would agree about how our country works best. Politicians and the media would see the great future that you see.

We make decisions every day in our lives. You may hear negative people say that things can never be great again in

America. Some people will complain and sound hopeless. They're wrong. Business solutions can provide great jobs. And business solutions usually don't involve millions of pages of government rules!

We want millions of businesses working to solve problems and employ people every day. With good government, and millions of business owners working on job creation, our country can thrive like never before.

Shouldn't we want to help make the United States the best place to do business in the world? Wouldn't that help the most workers to do well and provide for their families? If we do this right, everybody who wants a good job can get a good job. Can you see how everybody wins? If you understand this, you will understand capitalism.

Someday you may travel the world. You may have an opportunity to see how people do in countries without capitalism and freedom. Compare these countries with our country. Chances are, people in our country will have much, much higher standards of living.

It's very simple. Capitalism has been an engine which helped lift most people up in our country. It led to hundreds of millions of opportunities, including the opportunity (and resources) to help people who needed help.

Like business people, we should be willing to fight for our future and to be optimistic about it. America is not perfect, but we love our country, knowing it can be the greatest land of opportunity in the world. We will succeed with freedom, capitalism, hard work, and good government.

With your choice, working and speaking together, we can help create new opportunities across the country. People who don't agree with us now might even thank us when we're through. They might get better jobs than they ever dreamed of, partly because of you!

Are you ready to teach capitalism to America? Let's help lift up the people around us and show them how we can achieve Our Best Tomorrow!

Acknowledgments

Once again, our family pitched in on this book. I knew I was getting good feedback when family members suggested that Lauren needed to edit and change my work.

Most significantly, we summoned to duty two distinguished teachers in our family - Cynthia Branstetter and Cheryl Martin. Cindy and Cheryl reviewed the book and offered suggestions to help us connect with students. They helped us with other editing as well. My parents, Bob and Patsy Hudson, offered their blessings and input, as always.

Special thanks to my dad, our patriarch, who taught me just about everything I know about capitalism. As you can see from his illustrations, Dad is a terrific artist. Dad turned to art as he grew up in a family which had few creature comforts. Mom and Dad, and my wife Melissa's mom and dad, lived so many aspects of the American dreams told in *Our Best Tomorrow*. We're eternally grateful they paved the way for us.

I would never have authored the first book or co-authored this one without the help and encouragement of Authors Rick Robinson and Bob Schrage, two of the finest friends, fathers and community servants you could ever meet. Artist Kevin Kelly volunteered so much of his time in promoting the first book and then, as always, hit the right cord for the cover art on this book. Kevin Kelly and photographer Jymi Bolden make a great team – consider using them for your next book cover!

You can't practice law and write a book each year without a wonderful partner in life and children who make good decisions. Melissa's love and support means everything. Our 17 year old son Robbie is a kind, generous young man who, remarkably, usually puts his family's joy above his. Not your typical teenager.

Finally, what can I say about my daughter Lauren? With the business fables in this book, you have read her work, not mine. I threw a few ideas in there, but we changed very little of what she wrote. She wrote quickly, naturally, and met her deadline. Her text needed less editing than mine. I'm not sure how I feel about that. We finally have a true writer in the family. She's 13 years old.

God willing, a book on American exceptionalism, a return to my roots with a book entitled *The Management Counselor*, and another book of pro-business columns will follow. Thanks to all of our friends and clients who helped with the first book and this one. Because of you, I'll get to keep writing briefs and legal letters for a living, while writing books for fun at night and on weekends.

About The Authors

Robert D. Hudson

Rob is an attorney and owner of the law firm Frost Brown Todd, LLC, representing businesses in the firm's labor and employment law practice group. Rob has been immersed in his region's economic development for over two decades. He helped lead Northern Kentucky's two largest business organizations, as Chair of the Northern Kentucky Chamber of Commerce and the Covington Business Council. He served as President of the Northern Kentucky Society for Human Resources Management, President for Be-Concerned, Inc., President of the University of Kentucky Alumni Association in Greater Cincinnati, and as a Board Member for the Tri-County Economic Development Corporation.

Rob authored *A Better Tomorrow – Fighting for Capitalism and Jobs in the Heartland*, which chronicled President Obama's first term in office from the perspective of a common sense business leader. The book became an Amazon #1 Hot New Release for Political Economy Books and an Amazon Bestseller. *A Better Tomorrow* received the Silver Medal at the 2013 National E-Lit Book Awards. The New York Book Festival selected it as one of 2013's top business books. Rob has also authored hundreds of pro-business columns for various publications.

A frequent lecturer and trainer on business, legal and leadership topics, Rob has been recognized as a Best Lawyer in America, Kentucky Super Lawyer, Cincy Leading Lawyer, and by Chambers and Partners as the "go to employment lawyer in Northern Kentucky." He has been inducted into the Taking Care of Business Hall of Fame and is a past recipient of the Area Development District's Outstanding Community Leadership Award. Rob served as a regular co-host for the television show "Leading Businesses, Leading Communities." He recently received the Northern Kentucky Frontiersman Award for lifetime achievement in serving businesses.

Rob met his wife-to-be, then Melissa Martin, at the University of Kentucky in 1980. After receiving a B.S. in Accounting with High Distinction, Rob graduated from the University of Kentucky College of Law and moved to Greater Cincinnati. Rob and Melissa reside in Villa Hills, Kentucky with their two children, Robbie (age 17) and, of course, Lauren (age 13). Rob and Robbie coached youth athletics at Lakeside Christian Church for many years, where they taught Kentucky's two gospels simultaneously – faith and basketball.

Lauren Hudson

Lauren, a student at Turkeyfoot Middle School in Northern Kentucky, wrote the fiction portions of this book over her 2013 summer break. Lauren is a Duke Scholar and has received a wide range of awards for academic achievement. Lauren has been recognized for her writing talent, having been selected from the Northern Kentucky region to compete in state writing contests. She also serves on the Turkeyfoot Student Council.

A gifted presenter and actor, Lauren has received statewide recognition in Forensics speech and drama competitions, with starring roles in her school's last several drama productions. Lauren plays the piano and was a member of the Kentucky State Honor Choir, performing in the Kentucky Center for the Performing Arts.

In 2011, Lauren presented a business speech to the Northern Kentucky Chamber, receiving a standing ovation. *The Community Recorder* and nky.com have featured Lauren repeatedly in stories about her leadership and versatility in academic and extracurricular activities.

Lauren is also a talented scholar athlete. From the guard position, she led Turkeyfoot Middle School in scoring on the basketball court over the last two seasons. Lauren plays Elite Soccer for Kings-Hammer in Greater Cincinnati. Most recently, she started center-mid for Dixie High School Junior Varsity squad, leading the team in scoring as an 8th grader.